Access Granted

~ Ethan L. Ketterer ~

Author's Note

Writing ***Access Granted*** was more than a project—it was a journey through the many **"no's"** I've encountered in my own life. Each rejection, each delay, and every moment of confusion became a stepping stone to understanding that God's divine timing is always better than my own.

This book isn't just a collection of encouragements—it's a testimony. It's filled with pages I once cried over, chapters I once lived, and prayers I once prayed in silence. If you've ever felt overlooked, forgotten, or stuck behind a closed door, know that this book was written with you in mind.

The stories and scriptures inside are meant to meet you where you are and gently lead you to a place of renewed hope and deeper faith. It's okay to question. It's okay to feel disappointed. But don't unpack and stay there. My prayer is that this book helps you see the power in the pause, the beauty in the denial, and the purpose in the waiting.

Thank you for picking up this book. Thank you for allowing me to speak into your life. And most of all, thank you for choosing to believe that access isn't just granted to others—it's coming for you too.

With expectation and gratitude,

Ethan L. Ketterer

Dedication

To every soul who ever sat in front of a locked door, praying it would open...

To those who've battled through rejections, delays, detours, and disappointments. This is for the ones who stood silently in rooms full of people being celebrated, wondering if anyone would ever see their worth.

To the person who watched others walk into opportunities they prayed for, and still chose to clap through their tears—this book is for you.

For the ones who stayed faithful when it felt like nothing was happening, who kept believing even when the evidence said otherwise, and who chose trust over bitterness...

- **You are not forgotten.**
- **You are not overlooked.**
- **You are simply being positioned.**

Your ***"Access Granted"*** moment is not just coming—it's already been written by the Author of your story.

May these pages remind you that every **“no”** was just preparation for a better **“yes.”** And when the door opens... walk boldly through it.

—**Ethan L. Ketterer**

Optional Book Signing Page

This copy of ***Access Granted*** was signed with love and gratitude.

To: ______________________________________

Date: ____________________________________

Signature: ________________________________

Message:

____

____

____

____

Thank you for being part of this journey. May your life be filled with open doors and divine favor.

Table of Contents

Chapter 1: When Doors Slam Shut

Scripture:

"What he opens no one can shut, and what he shuts no one can open." —Revelation 3:7 **(NIV)**

Chapter Overview:

This chapter begins your journey through rejection and spiritual realignment. It invites the reader to confront the pain of closed doors—moments that sting, confuse, and disappoint—but reframes them as divine interventions, necessary for guidance, growth, and God's ultimate plan.

Chapter Content:

There's something deafening about the sound of a door slamming shut when you were sure it was meant to open. The job interview you nailed, only to get the rejection email. The friendship you poured into, only to be ghosted. The opportunity you prayed for, only to watch it pass you by.

The sound of that door closing hits deep. It's not just about the opportunity—it's about your heart, your hope, your belief that ***maybe this was it***. And when it's not, the questions come in like waves.

God, didn't I trust You? Didn't I prepare? Didn't I pray with all I had? Why would You allow it to slip through my fingers?

Here's what I've learned: closed doors aren't signs of failure—they're signs of God's favor. Yes, ***favor.*** Because He loves you too much to let you walk into a room that wasn't designed to hold your calling.

A closed door might mean the timing is off, or the opportunity would distract you from purpose. It could mean that there's something or someone behind that door that would wound you, not welcome you. And God, in His mercy, says no.

Rejection feels like punishment, but in the hands of God, it's often protection.

You can't always see what He's saving you from, but that's what trust is. It's choosing to believe that God is good, even when the outcome wasn't.

I've stood in front of slammed doors with tears in my eyes and doubt in my heart. But I've also looked back months—even years—later and thanked God for the very thing that once broke me. Why? Because He had a better door. A prepared door. A divine appointment that wouldn't have happened if I had forced my way through the wrong one.

If you're standing at a closed door right now, I want to encourage you: it's okay to feel the disappointment, but don't camp there. Don't let that slam echo so loud that you miss the knock of the next open door God is bringing your way.

You may not see it today, but trust this—God doesn't close a door unless He's preparing a better one. And when He opens it? No one, no situation, no rejection can shut it.

Key Points:

- A closed door is not a closed future.
- God's **"no"** is often protection, not punishment.
- Redirection is part of divine alignment.
- Delays and denials refine your dependence on God.
- What feels like the end may actually be the start of something greater.

Reflection Questions:

1. What is one door you prayed would open that didn't—and how did you respond?
2. Looking back, can you now see God's hand in that closed opportunity?
3. How have your past **"no's"** shaped your faith or redirected your path?
4. What emotions come up when you face rejection? How do you usually process them?
5. Is there a door you're still standing in front of, refusing to walk away?
6. Can you recall a time when God's **"no"** made way for a better **"yes"?**

Prayer to End the Chapter

Father, thank You for every door You closed that I didn't understand. Even when I felt hurt or confused, You were working for my good. Help me to release what wasn't for me and walk boldly in faith toward what is. Strengthen my trust in Your plan. I know that when You say no, it's never without purpose. Prepare my heart for the access You've already ordained.

Amen.

Chapter 2: The Power of a "No"

Scripture:

"In their hearts humans plan their course, but the Lord establishes their steps." —Proverbs 16:9 **(NIV)**

Chapter Overview:

"No" is a word we often resist, but in the hands of God, it's not a rejection—it's a redirection. In this chapter, we explore the divine wisdom hidden inside the moments when God says **"no,"** and how those moments actually shape and strengthen us.

Chapter Content:

Hearing **"no"** never feels good. Whether it comes from people or from God, it often feels like denial, rejection, or even punishment. But what if "no" isn't God being distant—but God being deliberate?

We live in a world that worships immediate access, instant results, and open doors. We're taught that if we just try hard enough or believe big enough, we'll get a **"yes."** But that's not always how God operates. Sometimes, the most loving thing He can do is close a door and say, **"No—not this. Not now. Not here."**

God's **"no"** doesn't mean He's ignoring your prayers—it means He's answering them with better wisdom than you can currently understand. What feels like delay or denial may actually be divine protection.

In my own life, I've heard **"no"** when I was desperate for a **"yes."** I prayed, I believed, I pushed. But heaven stayed quiet, or worse—said no outright. And it wasn't until much later that I realized those no's were God's mercy, rerouting me toward purpose.

When we only look for God in the yes, we miss the profound lessons in the no. The **"no"** seasons mature us. They strip us of entitlement and strengthen our trust. They show us that God's plan isn't always to give us what we want, but to give us what we *need* to become who we were created to be.

God's **"no"** has purpose. ***It refines. It resets. It reroutes.***

Sometimes, the most powerful growth happens in the places where the doors didn't open, where the path was blocked, where the opportunity was withheld. It forces us to dig deeper, pray harder, and lean into a faith that isn't dependent on outcomes, but on obedience.

A **"no"** can also reveal our idols—things or people we've placed above God in our hearts. When He withholds something we've clung to, it's an invitation to return to Him as our source, not just our supplier.

Think about the moments when you've pushed and pushed for a yes. Have you ever gotten what you wanted only to realize it wasn't what you needed? God sees the end from the beginning. His no is not cruelty; it's careful craftsmanship. It's grace disguised as disappointment.

Trusting God in the no develops spiritual muscle. It creates room for character to grow, pride to be dismantled, and dependency on Him to deepen. Sometimes, God's best gifts are hidden in unanswered prayers.

So, the next time you hear **"no,"** don't assume God is shutting you out. Know that He is, instead, drawing you closer. Teaching you something deeper. Leading you to something greater.

Key Points:

- **"No"** is not rejection; it's redirection and protection.
- God's "no" is often the setup for a greater **"yes."**
- Trust is not proven in getting what you want, but in believing God even when you don't.
- Growth happens most during seasons of waiting and withheld access.

- God's no may reveal hidden idols and deepen trust.

Reflection Questions:

1. Can you remember a time when God's **"no"** disappointed you?
2. How did that experience shape your faith and perspective?
3. Are there current areas in your life where God may be saying **"not yet"** or **"no"?**
4. How do you typically react when your plans are interrupted?
5. What might God be protecting you from through that **"no"?**
6. Is there something you're pursuing more than God Himself?

Prayer to End the Chapter

Father, thank You for the **"no's"** I didn't want to hear but needed to receive. Thank You for protecting me from paths that were not meant for me, even when I didn't see the danger. Teach me to trust Your wisdom over my wants. Help me to believe that every **"no"** is preparing me for a greater **"yes."** Strengthen my faith in the quiet, in the waiting, and in the moments where I don't understand. I trust that You are guiding me to what's best.

Amen.

Chapter 3: I Thought That Was My Door

Scripture:

"'For my thoughts are not your thoughts, neither are your ways my ways,' declares the Lord." —Isaiah 55:8 **(NIV)**

Chapter Overview:

This chapter explores the heartbreak and confusion that comes with believing a door was meant for you—only to see it close. We'll dive into the emotional aftermath of misplaced expectations and the divine redirection that follows when God gently says, "That wasn't your door."

Chapter Content:

You prayed about it. You fasted for it. You saw all the signs and believed with your whole heart that it was *your* door. It made sense. It aligned with your skills, your desires, and even your prayers. You thought it was your season, your opportunity, your breakthrough.

And then the door closed.

Few things feel more disorienting than believing something was yours, only to discover it wasn't. The emotional whiplash can leave you feeling misled, even betrayed—like God changed the plan without informing you. But in those moments of pain and confusion, there's an opportunity to trust on a deeper level.

Sometimes what we thought was our door was really a distraction. It looked good. It felt good. It even appeared to have God's fingerprints on it. But good and God aren't always the same thing.

God doesn't just open doors that are convenient—He opens doors that are ***consecrated***. And sometimes that means closing the ones that were never meant for us, no matter how much we wanted them.

We often assume that the things that feel right are automatically God-ordained. But feelings can be misleading. God works on a deeper level—He sees what we can't. He knows the full picture. And in His mercy, He closes doors we were never equipped or destined to walk through.

It's possible to mistake emotional attachment for divine confirmation. We get attached to outcomes. We build stories in our heads. We picture ourselves walking through certain doors with joy and celebration. And when those doors don't open, it can feel like something's been stolen from us.

- But what if that door wasn't the blessing—but the burden?
- What if it would have pulled you out of alignment with your purpose?
- What if the delay was divine and the closed door was a shield?

Letting go doesn't mean you've failed. It means you're making space. Space for the ***right*** door. The one with your name on it. The one that leads to joy without compromise. The one that won't require you to shrink who you are to fit where you don't belong.

And when that door opens, it won't take striving. It won't leave you questioning your worth. It will open with peace, clarity, and the unmistakable signature of God's hand.

Key Points:

- Just because something looks right doesn't mean it's God's will.
- Disappointment often precedes redirection.
- Misplaced expectations can become divine setups for realignment.
- The door that didn't open wasn't yours—and that's okay.
- Emotional attachment doesn't equal divine assignment.

Reflection Questions:

1. Have you ever been convinced that something was yours, only to watch it fall apart?
2. How did you process the emotional fallout of that disappointment?
3. Looking back, can you see how God may have protected you by closing that door?
4. What are you still holding onto that God might be asking you to release?
5. How can you shift from disappointment to trust?
6. Are there any current opportunities you're forcing that may not be God's best for you?

Prayer to End the Chapter

Lord, I confess that I've grieved over doors I thought were mine. I've questioned Your timing and doubted Your voice. But today, I choose to trust You. I release every expectation that doesn't align with Your will. Help me to stop chasing what's not mine and start waiting on what You've prepared for me. Thank You for closing doors that would have led me away from Your best. I believe what You have for me is still ahead.

Amen.

Chapter 4: Delayed but Not Denied

Scripture:

"For the revelation awaits an appointed time; it speaks of the end and will not prove false. Though it linger, wait for it; it will certainly come and will not delay." —Habakkuk 2:3 **(NIV)**

Chapter Overview:

Waiting is one of the hardest parts of the faith journey. This chapter unpacks the beauty of divine delay and reminds the reader that delay does not equal denial. What seems like a detour may actually be preparation for the door God is building.

Chapter Content:

There's a particular kind of frustration that comes from being ready—heart, mind, and spirit—and still having to wait. When you've done everything you know to do. When you've stood in faith. When you've prepared, praised, and positioned yourself. And yet... nothing moves.

You're not denied. You're delayed. And there's a difference.

Denial says it's not happening. Delay says it's not happening *yet.* The word ***yet*** holds power. It implies process. It implies timing. It implies that something is happening behind the scenes, even if you can't see it yet.

In Scripture, we constantly see people walking through seasons of delay. David was anointed king long before he sat on the throne. Joseph had a dream, but found himself in a pit and a prison before reaching the palace. Even Jesus waited 30 years before stepping into His public ministry.

Delay is not punishment—it's preparation. It's the classroom of character. It's the wilderness where faith is formed and trust is tested. God is not trying to wear you down—He's trying to build you up.

There are things God is working out ***in you*** **and** ***around you*** that must be completed before the door opens. What if you got the opportunity but lacked the maturity? What if you stepped through too soon and mishandled what God meant to bless?

Delays also test your consistency. Will you still worship while you wait? Will you keep sowing seeds of faith when there's no immediate harvest? Will you maintain integrity and humility even when no one is watching?

Sometimes, delay feels like a wilderness. But remember, it was in the wilderness that Moses was called, Elijah heard God's whisper, and Jesus prepared for His ministry. The wilderness isn't just a waiting room—it's a training ground.

God often does His greatest work in you before He does His greatest work through you. So while you wait, trust that you are being equipped. Every tear, every unanswered question, every quiet moment—it's all building something in you that a quick breakthrough could never produce.

If you're in a season where it feels like everything is paused—take heart. Heaven hasn't forgotten you. God is still moving. And the delay is not a detour—it's divine.

You're not waiting in vain. You're waiting with purpose.

Key Points:

- Delay is not denial; it's preparation for what's coming.
- God's timing is always perfect, even when it doesn't align with our expectations.
- Many biblical heroes experienced delays before destiny.
- Faith is refined in the waiting.
- The wilderness is not wasted—it's where purpose is shaped.

Reflection Questions:

1. Are you currently in a season of delay?
2. What has God been teaching you while you wait?
3. Have you mistaken delay for denial in any area of your life?
4. How can you shift your perspective from frustration to faith?
5. What can you do while you wait that will prepare you for what's next?
6. How are you maintaining your faith, focus, and obedience during the delay?

Prayer to End the Chapter

God, I thank You for the delay—even when I don't understand it. Help me to see it not as a punishment but as preparation. Strengthen my faith when I grow weary. Remind me that You are never late and that everything You've promised will come to pass in Your perfect time. Help me to wait well. I believe that what You have for me is still on the way.

Amen.

Chapter 5: Watching Others Walk In

Scripture:

"Let us not become weary in doing good, for at the proper time we will reap a harvest if we do not give up." —Galatians 6:9 (NIV)

Chapter Overview:

This chapter deals with one of the most difficult aspects of waiting on your own door—watching others walk through theirs. It speaks to the internal battle of jealousy, comparison, and quiet disappointment when it feels like everyone else is moving forward while you're standing still.

Chapter Content:

You celebrate them, but it stings.

You smile and clap and say all the right things, but deep down, you wonder—***when will it be my turn?*** You've watched friends get the promotions, family members get married, people online post highlight reels that feel like a cruel reminder of your own waiting season.

And while you want to be happy for them—and maybe you truly are—it doesn't erase the ache in your heart.

It's not that you're ungrateful. It's not that you're bitter. It's that you're human.

Watching others walk in while you're still standing in the hallway tests your heart in a way few things can. It reveals hidden insecurities. It challenges your endurance. And it calls you to a deeper level of trust.

God never asked you to ignore the ache. He asked you to bring it to Him. He knows how hard it is to keep showing up, keep believing, and keep cheering for others when your own breakthrough feels far away.

But here's what you need to remember: their door doesn't close yours. Their season isn't stealing your promise. What God has for *you* has your name on it. It won't go to someone else. It won't expire before you get to it. And when it opens, it will be right on time.

You are not being overlooked. You are being refined. And the person God is making you into during this season is someone who can walk through the door with character, grace, and gratitude—not comparison, resentment, or pride.

This is where your private character is shaped. When you can choose joy for someone else without compromising your hope. When you can praise God for someone else's miracle while holding space for your own.

Comparison is a thief, but contentment is a protector. It shields your mind from spiraling into jealousy and keeps your focus on what truly matters—God's faithfulness, not man's timelines.

Sometimes we're so focused on the doors others are walking through, we miss the one quietly opening for us in the background. God doesn't always make announcements. Sometimes, your door won't come with a spotlight—it'll come with peace.

You may find yourself asking, ***"Why them and not me?"*** But God invites you to flip the question: ***"What are You doing* in me *while I wait?"*** That shift in perspective moves your heart from envy to expectation.

Envy is loud, but trust is quiet. Trust doesn't always shout with confidence; sometimes it whispers through tears, "God, I still believe You haven't forgotten me."

Let those whispers be your anthem.

In the meantime, practice gratitude. Serve with joy. Rejoice sincerely. Because how you handle someone else's win is often preparation for how you'll steward your own.

Keep clapping. Keep showing up. Keep believing. Because the same God who opened the door for them is preparing one for you too.

Key Points:

- Someone else's breakthrough is not your setback.
- God's blessings for others don't cancel His plans for you.
- The waiting season refines your heart and deepens your faith.
- Your door will open in your divine time, not theirs.
- Contentment protects your heart from comparison and discouragement.
- Trust doesn't have to be loud to be real.

Reflection Questions:

1. How do you feel when others receive what you've been praying for?
2. Are there hidden feelings of jealousy or comparison that need to be surrendered to God?

3. What truths can you hold onto when it feels like everyone else is moving forward?
4. How can you authentically celebrate others while still holding hope for your own door?
5. What habits or thoughts do you need to change to wait well with grace?
6. Can you identify one area of your life where you need to grow in contentment?
7. What could God be developing in your character as you watch others walk in?

Prayer to End the Chapter

Lord, thank You for reminding me that what You've prepared for me cannot be taken by anyone else. Help me to celebrate others without comparison. Heal the parts of me that ache in silence. Strengthen my heart while I wait and guard my spirit from jealousy and discouragement. I trust that my time is coming. And until then, I will praise You in the hallway.

Amen.

Chapter 6: God, Why Not Me?

Scripture:

"Be still before the Lord and wait patiently for him; do not fret when people succeed in their ways, when they carry out their wicked schemes." —Psalm 37:7 **(NIV)**

Chapter Overview:

This chapter explores the raw emotion that surfaces when you feel like you've done everything right but are still waiting. It digs into the internal question: ***"God, why not me?"*** and brings clarity, comfort, and perspective to those who feel left out or forgotten.

Chapter Content:

You've followed God. You've prayed. You've done the work. You've kept your heart clean, your hands lifted, and your hope alive. Yet, the door remains closed.

Meanwhile, you see others—some who didn't even try as hard, some who mocked your faith, some who didn't even want the blessing—walk right into what you've been asking for.

It's hard not to ask the question: ***God, why not me?***

The weight of that question doesn't come from jealousy alone—it often stems from deep confusion, disappointment, and emotional fatigue. It's the silent cry of someone who's not trying to compare, but simply trying to understand.

And God can handle that cry.

Throughout the Bible, we see faithful men and women question God. Hannah cried bitterly for a child. Job wrestled with loss and confusion. David wept and asked, **"How long, Lord?"** These weren't moments of faithlessness—they were moments of honest relationship.

God doesn't silence your pain—He steps into it.

You may not realize it now, but sometimes the reason it hasn't happened yet is because God is writing a story that's bigger than the one you were praying for. His **"not yet"** isn't the end—it's the middle. It's the soil where endurance, wisdom, and humility grow.

When you cry, **"Why not me?"**—He whispers back, **"I haven't forgotten you."**

Jealousy grows in the soil of unanswered questions, but faith grows in the garden of surrender. When you surrender your timeline, your expectations, and your sense of fairness to God, you make room for peace.

You won't always get the answer you want—but you will get the strength you need.

And one day, you'll realize that what looked like delay was actually divine orchestration. That what felt like being overlooked was actually God preserving you for something bigger.

There's something sacred about the waiting room of heaven. It's a space that feels empty, but it's filled with unseen miracles in motion. It's where your character is strengthened, your patience is stretched, and your faith is purified.

Sometimes, the very people you envy have doors that come with unseen struggles. You're comparing your wait to someone else's walk, not knowing what burdens they carry on the other side. God's grace custom-fits your story. Your wait is purposeful. Your path is personalized.

You are not forgotten. You are not behind. You are not being punished. You are being prepared.

Your season is coming. Your moment will not be missed. And when it arrives, you'll walk through the door not with bitterness, but with testimony.

Key Points:

- **"Why not me?"** is an honest question that God can handle.
- God's delays are not His denials—they're setups for something greater.
- Surrender leads to peace, even when answers don't come quickly.
- Comparison feeds confusion, but faith restores clarity.
- Your story is still being written, and it's bigger than you think.
- Your wait is sacred, strategic, and filled with purpose.

Reflection Questions:

1. Have you recently asked God, **"Why not me?"** What triggered that question?
2. How can you express your pain without falling into comparison?
3. What truths can help you trust God even when others are receiving what you're praying for?

4. Are there areas in your life where you need to surrender expectations?
5. How might your current waiting season be preparing you for something greater?
6. What lies have you believed about your delay, and what truths can replace them?

Prayer to End the Chapter

God, I've cried out with questions I don't understand. I've wondered why it hasn't been my turn. But today, I choose to surrender my timelines and trust in Your divine plan. Remind me that You haven't forgotten me. Help me to wait without comparison, believe without bitterness, and rest in the truth that what You've prepared for me will come to pass. Strengthen me to celebrate others without doubting myself, and help me find joy even in the waiting. In Your perfect timing, I will walk through the door.

Amen.

Chapter 7: When Favor Feels Unfair

Scripture:

"Is it not lawful for me to do what I wish with what is my own? Or is your eye envious because I am generous?" —Matthew 20:15 (NASB)

Chapter Overview:

This chapter dives into the internal wrestling match that arises when God's favor seems to fall on others, especially when we feel more deserving or more faithful. It encourages readers to release the need to understand God's distribution of blessings and to focus on the truth that His grace is personal, intentional, and always purposeful.

Chapter Content:

It's hard when it looks like God is handing out miracles like confetti, and none of it is landing on you.

You're not trying to be bitter. You're trying to be grateful. But watching people walk into open doors, receive blessings you prayed for, and overflow with favor when you feel dry—it can wear on your spirit.

You ask, **"What did I miss? What more could I have done?"**

The truth is—nothing.

The parable of the workers in **Matthew 20** tells us something powerful: the landowner paid everyone the same, no matter when they showed up to work. Some came early. Some came late. But all were blessed.

The ones who came early grumbled—not because they weren't paid—but because someone else received the same reward with what looked like less effort.

Favor is never about fairness. Favor is about the Father's heart.

God doesn't bless based on seniority or perceived worth. He blesses based on His sovereignty. His ways are higher, His plan deeper. And when He blesses someone else, it doesn't mean He skipped you—it means He's still working.

We often equate God's favor with our own sense of merit. We think, ***"I've served longer. I've prayed harder. I've remained faithful."*** But grace doesn't follow human logic. It breaks the rules of meritocracy and reminds us that God's blessings are rooted in love, not labor.

When favor feels unfair, it's an invitation to recalibrate our perspective. God's generosity isn't a reflection of who deserves what—it's a reflection of who He is.

It takes maturity to rejoice in someone else's favor while still holding onto faith for your own. It takes courage to clap when your heart is hurting and to praise when your hope feels thin.

But that posture is powerful. That posture is preparation.

Because when your time comes, your heart will be clean. Your faith will be deep. And your praise won't be poisoned with comparison.

And remember, we don't always see the full cost of someone else's blessing. The spotlight often hides the struggle. The promotion you envied may come with pressure you weren't ready for. The relationship you longed for may be a storm in disguise. God sees beyond the surface. He blesses in the fullness of truth.

God's generosity toward others is not a threat to you—it's a reminder that He's still in the business of blessing.

If He did it for them, He can do it for you. And when it's your time, you won't have to strive. The door will open. The favor will flow. And it will be just as personal, just as intentional, and just as fulfilling as it was meant to be.

Key Points:

- God's favor is not about fairness—it's about grace.
- Someone else's blessing is not your burden.
- Maturity is shown in how you respond to others' breakthroughs.
- God's timeline and measure of favor are not limited by human standards.
- Comparison obscures the full picture—only God sees what's truly good for us.

Reflection Questions:

1. Have you ever felt that God's blessings seemed unfair?
2. How do you typically respond when others are favored in areas where you're still waiting?
3. What can you learn from God's generosity toward others?
4. In what ways can you shift from comparison to celebration?
5. How has God shown you favor in ways you might have overlooked?
6. Are there unseen blessings in your life you've taken for granted?

Prayer to End the Chapter

Father, help me to release the need to understand Your ways and trust in Your heart. Teach me to celebrate others without comparison. Remove any bitterness, envy, or confusion that clouds my view of Your goodness. Remind me that Your favor is not a competition—it's a confirmation that You are near. Let my heart remain pure while I wait for what You've prepared for me. I trust You. I honor You. I will not measure Your goodness by someone else's story.

Amen.

Chapter 8: Healing from Comparison

Scripture:

"We do not dare to classify or compare ourselves with some who commend themselves. When they measure themselves by themselves and compare themselves with themselves, they are not wise." —2 Corinthians 10:12 **(NIV)**

Chapter Overview:

This chapter unpacks the trap of comparison and its subtle impact on our identity, confidence, and spiritual health. It invites the reader to trade comparison for contentment and insecurity for identity rooted in Christ.

Comparison is a silent thief. It doesn't barge in—it sneaks up on you in the quiet moments when you're scrolling through social media, attending a friend's celebration, or listening to someone else's testimony.

At first, it sounds like curiosity. Then it turns into criticism—of yourself.

- *Why isn't my life moving like theirs?*
- *Why don't I have what they have?*

- *What's wrong with me?*

Comparison never leads you toward purpose—it pulls you away from it. It's rooted in the fear that somehow you are not enough. That you've been overlooked. That maybe God is more generous with others than He is with you.

But here's the truth: you can't compare what God is doing in someone else's life to what He's building in yours. Different assignments come with different seasons. What they're walking in may be what you've prayed for—but your timeline is tailored by a God who knows you better than you know yourself.

Your story is not behind. It's on schedule.

Comparison isn't just about jealousy—it's often about doubt. Doubt in your value. Doubt in your timing. Doubt in your place in God's plan. But when you know your identity is rooted in Christ, you no longer have to chase affirmation through comparison—you walk in confidence, knowing that you are already chosen, already seen, already loved.

Healing from comparison doesn't mean you never notice what others are doing. It means you no longer use it as a measuring stick for your own worth or progress. It means you bless them and believe that your door is still coming.

Comparison says, **"There's not enough."**

Faith says, **"There's more than enough—for all of us."**

When you stop measuring your life against others, you start seeing your life through grace-colored lenses. You notice the doors that have opened. You recall the prayers that were answered. You begin to give thanks, not only for what is, but for what's coming.

The truth is, what's for you will never miss you. And what misses you was never meant to carry you. You are on a unique path, with a unique purpose, guided by a God who makes no mistakes.

There is no version of your story where God forgets you. He hasn't missed a moment. He hasn't skipped a page. And He certainly hasn't run out of favor with your name on it.

Key Points:

- Comparison is a distraction from your God-given purpose.
- Your story has its own timeline and divine appointments.
- Contentment flows from trusting God's individual plan for your life.
- Celebrating others doesn't diminish your own promise—it multiplies peace.

- Healing starts when you shift from measurement to gratitude.
- What's for you is protected, promised, and personalized by God.

Reflection Questions:

1. In what areas of life do you find yourself comparing most often?
2. How has comparison impacted your faith or confidence?
3. What truths from Scripture can help you combat feelings of inadequacy?
4. How can you practice contentment more intentionally this week?
5. Who can you celebrate today without comparison?
6. What would your life look like if you fully embraced your own pace?

Prayer to End the Chapter:

Lord, deliver me from the trap of comparison. Help me to see myself through Your eyes and to remember that my story is unfolding exactly as You designed it. Teach me to bless others without doubting myself, and to trust that You have good plans for me. Let contentment rise where comparison once lived. I believe my life is not behind—it's being beautifully written by You.

Amen.

Chapter 9: The Weight of Being Overlooked

Scripture:

"But the Lord said to Samuel, 'Do not consider his appearance or his height, for I have rejected him. The Lord does not look at the things people look at. People look at the outward appearance, but the Lord looks at the heart.'" —1 Samuel 16:7 **(NIV)**

Chapter Overview:

This chapter addresses the pain of being overlooked—by people, opportunities, or circumstances—and encourages the reader to trust that God sees, remembers, and is preparing a moment where their name will be called.

Chapter Content:

There's a deep ache that comes with being overlooked.

You were there. You showed up. You stayed faithful. But somehow, you were passed by.

When promotions were handed out, your name wasn't called. When leaders were chosen, you were left out. When blessings flowed, you were the one still waiting in the shadows.

Being overlooked makes you question your value. It tempts you to shrink back, to wonder if you're invisible not just to people—but to God.

But the same God who chose David from the field while everyone else focused on his older brothers sees *you* too.

David wasn't even invited to the lineup. His father didn't think he was significant enough. But God saw what no one else did. And when the moment came, David was anointed in front of everyone who had overlooked him.

There's something sacred about the silent seasons. The seasons where you're becoming, even if you're not being noticed. The truth is, God does His best work in hidden places—where ego can't grow and humility takes root.

You're not forgotten. You're being formed.

Sometimes being overlooked is the very space where your roots are digging deeper. When no one is applauding and no spotlight is shining, your faith is maturing, your confidence is being rebuilt, and your character is being refined.

It's in the quiet that we learn obedience. In the quiet, we learn to listen. In the quiet, we learn that it was never about being seen—it was always about being ***ready***.

God has a habit of elevating the underestimated. He uses the rejected. He chooses the quiet ones in the background and gives them front row purpose. You are not invisible to heaven. Every sacrifice, every prayer, every act of obedience has been seen and noted.

And when the time is right, you won't have to campaign for your name to be known. God will make the announcement. And the doors that remained locked for so long will swing open with grace and clarity.

The weight of being overlooked is real, but so is the One who sees. When God calls your name, no one can stop the oil from flowing. What's meant for you will find you—even if every door before it was locked.

So don't lose heart in the silence. Keep working. Keep believing. Keep trusting. Because the moment is coming where the silence will break, and the spotlight of God's timing will shine on you—not because you pushed your way into the room, but because God opened the door.

Key Points:

- Being overlooked by people doesn't mean you're forgotten by God.
- Hidden seasons are often preparation for public purpose.
- God calls and qualifies in His own time, and His timing is always perfect.
- Your significance isn't defined by man's recognition.
- Silence is not absence; it is preparation in disguise.

Reflection Questions:

1. Have you experienced a time when you felt overlooked or invisible?
2. How did that experience shape your confidence or faith?
3. What truths from God's Word can ground you when you feel unseen?
4. How can you use hidden seasons as preparation for your future?
5. What would it look like to fully trust God's timing and validation?
6. Are you building your life to be noticed or to be ready?

Prayer to End the Chapter:

God, I admit that being overlooked hurts. I've wrestled with feeling unseen and undervalued. But today, I anchor myself in the truth that You see me. You know my heart, my work, my faithfulness—and none of it is wasted. Strengthen me to stay faithful in the quiet places, and prepare me for the moment when You call my name. I trust that You have not forgotten me. I will not chase applause—I will pursue obedience.

Amen.

Chapter 10: Refining in the Waiting Room

Scripture:

"But they who wait for the Lord shall renew their strength; they shall mount up with wings like eagles; they shall run and not be weary; they shall walk and not faint." —Isaiah 40:31 **(ESV)**

Chapter Overview:

This chapter explores the sacred, refining process that occurs while we wait. It focuses on how the waiting room is not a holding place, but a training ground for character, clarity, and calling.

Chapter Content:

Waiting has a reputation for being passive, frustrating, and stagnant—but in God's economy, waiting is one of the most active seasons of spiritual growth you'll ever experience.

There is a reason the Bible talks so much about waiting. Because what happens in the waiting room isn't about what you're waiting ***for***—it's about what God is doing ***in you***.

Waiting exposes your priorities. Waiting tests your attitude. Waiting reveals what you believe about God's timing, goodness, and promises.

It's in the waiting room where impatience meets purpose, and where you learn that delay isn't denial—it's development.

God never wastes waiting.

Think about it—Moses waited in the wilderness before leading. Joseph waited in prison before reigning. Jesus waited in obscurity before ministry. Waiting isn't a punishment—it's a preparation.

In the waiting room, God prunes what cannot go with you into the next season. He sheds distractions, reshapes identity, and roots you deeper in Him.

This is where humility is nurtured, where entitlement is removed, and where gratitude is cultivated.

It's easy to get frustrated when you feel stuck. But what if you're not stuck—you're being ***stilled*?**

Stillness isn't absence of motion. It's the intentional surrender of your pace to the rhythm of God's will. In stillness, your vision clears. In stillness, your ears tune to His whisper. In stillness, your foundation strengthens.

The waiting room can feel like the loneliest place on earth—especially when others seem to be moving forward. But what if your wait is your witness? What if how you wait becomes the testimony that encourages someone else to endure?

Your character is being formed in obscurity. Your motives are being checked in silence. Your endurance is being stretched in delay. But none of it is in vain. God is working behind the curtain while you're seated in the hallway.

There is breakthrough in the wait. There is power in the pause. There is glory in the delay.

When you emerge from the waiting room, you won't be the same person who walked in. You'll be wiser, stronger, more patient, and more equipped. Because while others saw you as idle, God was sharpening you in secret.

And when your name is called, when your door swings open, you'll walk through not only with preparation—but with purpose. You'll understand that the delay was the training ground for your destiny.

So don't despise the waiting room. Embrace it. Let it refine you. Let it ready you. Because when the door finally opens, you'll walk through it not just prepared—but transformed.

Key Points:

- Waiting is a place of spiritual refinement, not punishment.
- God uses waiting to develop strength, wisdom, and trust.
- Stillness allows us to hear and see God more clearly.
- Those who wait well are often the most prepared when the door opens.
- The wait often holds the key to your next level of purpose.

Reflection Questions:

1. How have you viewed the waiting seasons in your life up to this point?
2. What lessons or strengths have you gained during times of waiting?
3. In what ways has God used stillness to speak to or shape you?
4. Are there areas you're trying to rush that God may be refining?
5. How can you embrace the waiting room as a place of growth instead of frustration?

6. How has your time in the waiting room prepared you to encourage someone else?

Prayer to End the Chapter:

God, help me to stop resisting the waiting room and start receiving what You want to do in me here. Teach me to trust Your pace. Strip away what cannot go with me into the next season. Sharpen my spirit and deepen my roots. Let the waiting refine me, not ruin me. I surrender my timeline for Your transformation. And when the time is right, help me walk out not just changed—but commissioned. **Amen.**

Chapter 11: Embracing the Unseen

Scripture:

"For I know the plans I have for you, declares the Lord, plans for welfare and not for evil, to give you a future and a hope." — Jeremiah 29:11 **(ESV)**

Chapter Overview:

This chapter explores the mystery and beauty of stepping into what is not yet visible. It emphasizes that faith often requires us to trust in a divine plan that unfolds beyond our natural sight, inviting us to welcome the unseen with courage and hope.

Chapter Content:

Sometimes, the path ahead appears cloaked in uncertainty—a vast unknown that challenges our need for immediate clarity. Yet, in that very obscurity, God is revealing His master plan for your life.

When we choose to embrace the unseen, we are not acting on blind hope, but on the certainty of a promise. Every step taken in faith is a testimony of trust; every leap into uncertainty becomes an opportunity for divine intervention.

Just as the early believers stepped out in faith without knowing the outcome, you are invited to walk confidently into the mystery of God's timing. The unseen is not a void—it is the canvas on which God paints the masterpiece of your destiny.

In these moments, doubt may whisper its familiar refrain. But consider the examples of those who ventured into the unknown: Abraham left his familiar grounds, David faced giants with nothing but trust, and countless others have witnessed the miraculous when they surrendered to divine guidance.

Embracing the unseen is about understanding that what is hidden is often where the greatest treasures reside. It is the space where transformation happens, where your character is sharpened, and where hope is renewed. In the silence of the unknown, God speaks louder than any certainty you have ever known.

Key Points:

- The unseen is not emptiness but a realm of divine possibility.
- Faith calls us to step forward even when the destination is not clear.
- Trusting God in uncertainty unlocks doors to unexpected blessings.

- Every moment of the unknown is an invitation to deepen your reliance on God's promises.
- The mystery of the unseen nurtures spiritual growth and character development.

Reflection Questions:

1. How do you respond when faced with uncertainty or an unseen future?
2. What experiences have taught you to trust beyond what you can see?
3. In what ways has stepping into the unknown deepened your faith?
4. How can embracing the unseen become a source of strength rather than fear?
5. What steps can you take to invite God's presence into your moments of uncertainty?

Prayer to End the Chapter:

Lord, help me to find courage in the midst of uncertainty. Teach me to trust in the plans You have laid out, even when the path ahead is hidden. May I step boldly into the unknown, secure in Your promises and open to the wonders You are orchestrating in my life. Transform my fear into faith and my doubts into declarations of trust. Amen.

Chapter 12: Walking in Faith's Footsteps

Scripture:

"Trust in the Lord with all your heart, and do not lean on your own understanding." —Proverbs 3:5 **(ESV)**

Chapter Overview:

This chapter delves into the journey of following ***faith*** over sight. It illustrates how stepping into the footsteps of those who have gone before us builds a bridge between our present struggles and future victories.

Chapter Content:

Walking in ***faith*** means choosing a path that isn't always visible but is paved by divine guidance. It calls for relinquishing control and trusting that every step, no matter how small, is part of God's master design.

Reflect on the footprints of biblical heroes—each moment of obedience, each act of trust, and every quiet surrender paved the way for a legacy of faith. Their lives remind us that walking in faith is less about perfection and more about perseverance.

As you take each ***step***, you are not alone. The presence of the Almighty goes before you, guiding your steps, steadying your pace, and softening the hard ground beneath your feet. In moments of uncertainty, recall that the journey of faith is a mosaic of both triumphs and trials that ultimately mold you into a beacon of hope.

Key Points:

- Walking in ***faith*** requires trust beyond what we can see.
- Our footsteps are guided by the legacy of those who walked before us.
- Each step, whether small or bold, is part of God's unfolding plan.
- Perseverance in ***faith*** builds resilience and deepens our spiritual walk.
- Embracing the journey transforms our struggles into testimonies.

Reflection Questions:

1. How have the footsteps of past ***faith*** heroes inspired your own journey?

2. In what ways do you find strength when the path seems unclear?
3. What small steps of ***faith*** have led to big breakthroughs in your life?
4. How can you lean more on God's guidance in your everyday walk?
5. What can you do to encourage others to take their own steps of faith?

Prayer to End the Chapter:

Heavenly Father, as I set out on this journey of ***faith***, may my steps be guided by Your wisdom and love. Help me trust You with all my heart, even when the path is hidden. Strengthen my resolve to walk in Your footsteps, and let my journey inspire others to follow Your light. Amen.

Chapter 13: Unleashing the Power of Surrender

Scripture:

"Submit yourselves therefore to God. Resist the devil, and he will flee from you." —James 4:7 **(ESV)**

Chapter Overview:

This chapter reveals how true strength is found in ***surrender***. It challenges the notion that surrender is weakness, showing instead that yielding to God's will is the ultimate act of empowerment.

Chapter Content:

Surrender is often misunderstood as defeat, yet it is the courageous act of letting go and trusting God's plan. It is in surrendering our own agendas that we unlock divine breakthroughs.

When we release the burden of control, we open ourselves to receive grace, wisdom, and unexpected strength. Like a seed that must break before new life can emerge, ***surrender transforms limitations into opportunities for growth.***

Consider the moments when surrender has reshaped your life—each time you yielded control, God revealed His power in ways that surpassed your understanding. In this act of divine exchange, our weaknesses become platforms for His strength to shine through.

Key Points:

- Surrender is an act of courage, not a sign of weakness.
- Letting go creates space for divine intervention.
- True strength emerges when we yield our own control.
- God's plan often unfolds beautifully when we relinquish our need to direct every outcome.
- Surrender transforms our limitations into opportunities for growth.

Reflection Questions:

1. What does surrender mean to you in your personal journey?
2. How have you experienced strength through yielding to God's plan?
3. When have you noticed God's power manifest in your moments of weakness?
4. What areas of your life are you holding on to that need surrender?

5. How can you cultivate a spirit of openness to divine guidance?

Prayer to End the Chapter:

Lord, teach me the beauty of surrender. Help me release the need for control and to trust fully in Your perfect plan. May my weaknesses become the soil where Your strength grows, and may I always be open to the transformative power of yielding to Your will. Amen.

Chapter 14: Cultivating a Heart of Gratitude

Scripture:

"Give thanks in all circumstances; for this is the will of God in Christ Jesus for you." —1 Thessalonians 5:18 **(ESV)**

Chapter Overview:

This chapter centers on the transformative power of ***gratitude***. It explores how a grateful heart can transform ordinary moments into divine appointments, fueling joy and resilience even in the midst of adversity.

Chapter Content:

Gratitude is not merely an emotion—it's a way of life. It shifts our perspective, turning challenges into lessons and ordinary days into blessings. When we nurture a heart of gratitude, we unlock a wellspring of joy that transcends circumstances.

Reflect on the moments that have challenged you, and see them as opportunities for growth. Gratitude transforms trials into triumphs by revealing the hidden blessings within every experience.

In a world quick to focus on what is missing, choose instead to celebrate what is present. Let each day be a canvas painted with the colors of thankfulness, inspiring a spirit that radiates hope, peace, and unwavering trust in God's goodness.

Key Points:

- A grateful heart transforms perception and experience.
- Thankfulness turns challenges into opportunities for growth.
- Gratitude is a daily practice that deepens our connection to God's blessings.
- Each moment offers a hidden blessing waiting to be recognized.
- A life of gratitude inspires resilience, joy, and a profound sense of purpose.

Reflection Questions:

1. In what ways has gratitude changed your outlook on life?
2. What everyday blessings do you often overlook?
3. How can you cultivate a practice of thankfulness in your daily routine?
4. How has gratitude transformed your response to challenges?

5. What can you do today to express deeper gratitude for God's blessings?

Prayer to End the Chapter:

Gracious God, open my eyes to the abundance of Your blessings. Teach me to live each day with a heart overflowing with gratitude. May I find joy in every moment and recognize Your loving hand in all circumstances. Amen.

Chapter 15: Navigating the Storms of Life

Scripture:

"When you pass through the waters, I will be with you; and through the rivers, they shall not overwhelm you." —Isaiah 43:2 **(ESV)**

Chapter Overview:

This chapter addresses the inevitable ***storms*** we encounter in life. It offers guidance on how to remain anchored in faith, even when turbulent winds threaten to uproot us.

Chapter Content:

Storms come in many forms—loss, uncertainty, and overwhelming challenges. Yet, in these moments of fierce trial, God's presence is most evident. Just as a lighthouse stands firm amid crashing waves, His light guides us through even the darkest tempests.

These trials are not designed to break us but to remind us of our resilient spirit. In every storm, there is a lesson waiting to be learned, a strength waiting to be discovered. Even as the winds howl and the rain pounds, trust that God is crafting a safe harbor within you.

Every challenge refines your character, testing your resolve and deepening your faith. ***In the heart of the storm, cling to the promises of God, knowing that His grace is a shelter that will never falter.***

Key Points:

- Storms are opportunities for spiritual growth and resilience.
- God's presence provides shelter and guidance in times of trouble.
- Every trial refines and strengthens our character.
- Trusting in God transforms chaos into a journey of hope.
- Amid the fiercest storms, divine assurance anchors our soul.

Reflection Questions:

1. What storms have shaped your spiritual journey?
2. How do you find strength during life's most challenging moments?
3. In what ways has God's presence been a refuge in your times of trial?

4. How can you transform your perspective on challenges into opportunities for growth?
5. What steps can you take to anchor yourself more firmly in God during turbulent times?

Prayer to End the Chapter:

Lord, when the storms of life rage around me, be my refuge and strength. Help me to see each challenge as an opportunity to grow in faith and resilience. Anchor my soul in Your everlasting promises, and let Your light guide me through every tempest. Amen.

Chapter 16: Anchored in His Promises

Scripture:

"Let us hold fast the confession of our hope without wavering, for He who promised is faithful." —Hebrews 10:23 **(ESV)**

Chapter Overview:

This chapter emphasizes the importance of clinging to God's ***promises*** as our anchor in life. It explores how unwavering ***hope*** and trust in His Word can provide stability and assurance in uncertain times.

Chapter Content:

In a world where uncertainty often reigns, the promises of God stand as an unshakeable foundation. Anchoring yourself in these eternal truths is like mooring a ship against a storm—steady and secure.

Every promise in Scripture is a lifeline, assuring you that no matter the circumstances, ***God's word is true and His faithfulness endures forever.*** When doubts arise, let these promises remind you of a love that never fails and a plan that always prevails.

Living anchored in His promises means weaving them into the fabric of your daily life—**letting them shape your thoughts, your decisions, and your actions**. In doing so, you transform fear into hope and instability into unwavering faith.

Key Points:

- God's promises provide a stable foundation amid life's uncertainties.
- Clinging to Scripture transforms doubt into hope.
- Faith in His promises nurtures an unwavering spirit.
- Eternal truths become a guiding light in every situation.
- Anchoring in God's Word brings peace, strength, and assurance.

Reflection Questions:

1. Which of God's promises resonates most deeply with you?
2. How have His promises helped you overcome uncertainty?
3. In what ways can you incorporate His Word more fully into your daily routine?
4. How does anchoring in His promises change your perspective during challenging times?

5. What practical steps can you take to hold fast to these truths each day?

Prayer to End the Chapter:

Father, help me to remain anchored in Your eternal promises. When doubts assail me, let Your Word be the light that steadies my heart. Strengthen my hope and fortify my faith, that I might stand unshaken in the midst of life's uncertainties. Amen.

Chapter 17: The Art of Listening

Scripture:

"Know then that the Lord your God is God; he is the faithful God, keeping his covenant of love to a thousand generations of those who love him and keep his commandments." —Deuteronomy 7:9 **(ESV)**

Chapter Overview:

This chapter invites you to cultivate the art of listening—not only to God's whisper but also to the quiet wisdom that emerges from within. It underscores how attentive listening opens the door to deeper understanding and connection.

Chapter Content:

In the rush of life's noise, the art of listening is a divine practice. It requires quieting the clamor of everyday thoughts to hear the gentle, guiding voice of God. True listening is an active, intentional pursuit of truth and connection.

Listening deeply means more than hearing words—it's about understanding the unspoken, discerning the subtle signs, and recognizing God's presence in the silence. When you create space for genuine listening, you invite wisdom, comfort, and direction into your life.

As you practice this art, you begin to notice how both Scripture and life's quiet moments speak profound truths. The still, small voice that often goes unnoticed becomes the wellspring of divine guidance, transforming every encounter into a sacred dialogue.

Key Points:

- True listening requires intentional quiet and openness.
- Deep listening reveals both God's voice and inner wisdom.
- Practicing the art of listening enriches your spiritual connection.
- Silence often carries the most profound messages.
- Attentive listening transforms ordinary moments into sacred encounters.

Reflection Questions:

1. What steps can you take to cultivate a practice of deep listening in your life?
2. How have moments of silence provided guidance or insight for you?
3. In what ways does listening to God differ from simply hearing?
4. How can you create more space for quiet reflection in your day?

5. What has been the most meaningful message you've received in a moment of stillness?

Prayer to End the Chapter:

Lord, teach me the art of listening. In the stillness, may I hear Your gentle whisper and discern the quiet wisdom within me. Open my heart to receive Your guidance, and let every moment of silence become a sacred encounter with You. Amen.

Chapter 18: Rising Through Resilience

Scripture:

"Not only that, but we rejoice in our sufferings, knowing that suffering produces endurance, and endurance produces character, and character produces hope." —Romans 5:3-4 **(ESV)**

Chapter Overview:

This chapter celebrates resilience—the inner strength that emerges through trials and tribulations. It shows how each challenge becomes a stepping stone toward a stronger, more hopeful you.

Chapter Content:

Resilience is not the absence of hardship; it is the capacity to rise every time you fall. Through life's battles, you discover a reservoir of strength and hope that you never knew existed. ***Each trial, each setback, becomes an opportunity to build a character that is unbreakable.***

In every season of struggle, there is a hidden lesson that forges a new layer of endurance. Like a tree that bends but does not break in the storm, your spirit grows stronger with each challenge. ***Resilience transforms pain into purpose***, teaching you that every scar is a reminder of God's sustaining grace.

Let your heart be emboldened by the knowledge that your resilience is not built by circumstance alone, but by the gentle, persistent work of a loving God who refines you with every experience.

Key Points:

- Resilience is the strength to rise after every fall.
- Trials shape and strengthen your character.
- Each hardship carries a lesson that deepens your endurance.
- God's refining grace transforms pain into purpose.
- Resilience is a testimony of hope born out of struggle.

Reflection Questions:

1. What experiences have helped you develop resilience in your life?
2. How can you view setbacks as opportunities for growth?
3. In what ways has God's grace strengthened you during tough times?
4. How do you nurture a spirit of endurance in the midst of challenges?
5. What encouragement can you share with someone facing a difficult season?

Prayer to End the Chapter:

Gracious God, in my moments of struggle, remind me of the strength You have woven into my spirit. Help me to rise with resilience and transform every trial into a testimony of hope. May Your grace be the foundation that sustains me in every season. Amen.

Chapter 19: The Beauty of Redemption

Scripture:

"Therefore, if anyone is in Christ, he is a new creation. The old has passed away; behold, the new has come." —2 Corinthians 5:17 **(ESV)**

Chapter Overview:

This chapter celebrates the transformative beauty of redemption. It highlights how no matter the darkness of the past, God's redemptive love brings forth new beginnings and restores the broken into beauty.

Chapter Content:

Redemption is a powerful testimony of God's love—a journey from brokenness to wholeness. It is the divine act of restoring what was once lost, renewing hope, and breathing life into what seemed beyond repair.

Each story of redemption is a vivid reminder that the past does not define you. Through God's unfailing grace, every wound is healed and every regret transformed into a stepping stone toward a brighter future. In the light of redemption, scars become symbols of survival and proof of the transformative power of His love.

As you embrace the beauty of redemption, you not only reclaim your own narrative but also become a beacon of hope for others. Your testimony of renewal becomes an invitation for others to experience the liberating power of God's love.

Key Points:

- Redemption transforms past brokenness into new beginnings.
- God's love restores, heals, and renews our lives.
- Every scar can be a testimony of survival and grace.
- The beauty of redemption lies in the promise of continual renewal.
- Your journey of restoration can inspire hope in others.

Reflection Questions:

1. How has the experience of redemption transformed your life?
2. In what ways can you see God's hand in your journey from brokenness to wholeness?
3. What part of your past has been transformed by divine grace?
4. How can your story of redemption encourage others facing similar struggles?
5. What steps can you take to embrace new beginnings each day?

Prayer to End the Chapter:

Merciful God, thank You for the beauty of redemption that transforms my brokenness into hope. Help me to see each scar as a reminder of Your healing grace and to walk boldly into the new life You have prepared for me. May my story become a light that guides others toward Your redeeming love. Amen.

Chapter 20: Stepping into Destiny

Scripture:

"For we are his workmanship, created in Christ Jesus for good works, which God prepared beforehand, that we should walk in them." —Ephesians 2:10 **(ESV)**

Chapter Overview:

In this chapter, the focus shifts to embracing your destiny. It celebrates the journey of transformation you have experienced and calls you to step boldly into the purpose that God has intricately designed for your life.

Chapter Content:

Your destiny is not a distant dream but a present reality waiting to be claimed. Every moment of waiting, every step of faith, every trial and triumph has prepared you for this very moment. As you stand at the threshold of a new season, **God's call echoes clearly in your heart**.

Stepping into destiny means embracing both the lessons of the past and the promises of the future. It is an invitation to live out your purpose with courage, conviction, and a deep trust in the One who has guided your every step. You are not stepping forward alone;

every trial, every victory, and every silent moment of reflection has equipped you to fulfill the unique plan set before you.

Let this moment be a declaration of faith—a commitment to walk boldly into the destiny that awaits. Trust that each step is divinely orchestrated and that the journey ahead is filled with promise, purpose, and profound transformation.

Key Points:

- Your destiny is a culmination of every experience along your journey.
- Every step of faith prepares you for the purpose God has designed.
- Embracing destiny requires courage, trust, and a willing heart.
- The lessons of the past are the stepping stones to a future of promise.
- Walking into destiny is an act of surrender to God's perfect plan.

Reflection Questions:

1. How do you perceive the destiny God has prepared for you?
2. What experiences along your journey have shaped your readiness for the future?

3. In what ways can you actively step into the purpose set before you?
4. How does trusting in God's orchestration give you confidence to move forward?
5. What steps can you take today to embrace your destiny with boldness?

Prayer to End the Chapter:

Almighty God, I thank You for the journey that has brought me to the doorstep of my destiny. Strengthen my heart and embolden my spirit as I step into the purpose You have so lovingly prepared for me. May every step I take be a testament to Your grace and a reflection of Your divine plan. Guide me as I embrace the future with hope, courage, and unwavering faith. Amen.

Chapter 21: Living in Abundance

Scripture:

"And my God will supply every need of yours according to his riches in glory in Christ Jesus." —Philippians 4:19 (ESV)

Chapter Overview:

This chapter explores the idea that true abundance transcends material wealth and is rooted in the divine provision of God. It invites you to view each moment as an opportunity to experience His generosity and to recognize that every need is met in unexpected ways.

Chapter Content:

Imagine waking each day to a truth that every breath, every heartbeat, and every challenge is enveloped in divine grace. In the quiet moments of reflection, you come to understand that ***abundance is not measured by bank balances or possessions***, but by the overflowing love and provision of your Creator. When life presents obstacles—whether financial strain, emotional trials, or spiritual drought—you learn to see these moments as chances for God to demonstrate His care. Even when resources seem scarce, His promise remains: every need is anticipated, and every desire is known.

Throughout your journey, you may notice that the little blessings—an encouraging word from a friend, a sunrise that paints the sky in hues of hope, or a simple meal shared with gratitude—are pieces of a larger mosaic. They remind you that abundance is a state of mind and spirit. It's the ability to see the beauty in imperfection, to embrace the fullness of life even in its challenges, and to recognize that the divine economy operates on principles far beyond human measurement.

There is a quiet strength in accepting that what appears to be a lack is often a doorway to greater provision. In moments when your heart feels empty, let the words of an old proverb resonate: ***"Gratitude turns what we have into enough."*** This mindset transforms scarcity into an opportunity to trust and lean more fully into the promises of God. Each trial, then, becomes not a setback but a stepping stone towards a richer, more fulfilling existence.

As you journey forward, allow your soul to be open to the myriad ways God's blessings manifest. Whether through unexpected gifts, the warmth of a supportive community, or the resilience that emerges during hardships, abundance becomes a living testimony to divine generosity. In this season, you are invited to shift your focus from what is missing to what is present and overflowing. The very act of giving—sharing what little you have with others—further multiplies the blessings in your life, creating a ripple effect that enriches not only your own heart but also the lives of those around you.

Abundance is both a promise and a practice. It calls for an intentional posture of trust, an openness to receive, and a willingness to share generously. In every moment, there is the invitation to live fully, to celebrate the richness that lies in the ordinary, and to trust that your needs are not only known but lovingly provided for by the One who holds all things together.

Key Points:

- True abundance is defined by divine provision rather than material wealth.
- Every challenge can reveal hidden blessings and opportunities for growth.
- Gratitude transforms perception, turning scarcity into a testimony of God's generosity.
- Sharing and generosity multiply the blessings in our lives.

Reflection Questions:

1. In what ways have you experienced God's provision in unexpected circumstances?
2. How does adopting an attitude of gratitude change your perspective on scarcity?

3. What practical steps can you take to cultivate a spirit of generosity in your daily life?

Prayer to End the Chapter:

Lord, open my eyes to the abundance You provide in every moment. Teach me to trust in Your generosity and to see each challenge as an opportunity for growth and grace. May my heart overflow with gratitude and may I be a channel of Your love and provision to those around me. Amen.

Chapter 22: Discovering Your Unique Voice

Scripture:

"He has put a new song in my mouth, a hymn of praise to our God." —Psalm 40:3 **(ESV)**

Chapter Overview:

This chapter encourages you to uncover and celebrate the unique voice that God has bestowed upon you. It examines how expressing your true self through words, actions, and creativity is a powerful means to share hope and inspire transformation.

Chapter Content:

Deep within you lies a story—a narrative crafted by divine hands that is waiting to be expressed. Your voice, whether spoken, written, or even silent in the way you live, carries the imprint of God's creativity. It is a reflection of your innermost self, a blend of your experiences, dreams, and the gentle nudges of the Spirit. When you begin to recognize the power of your own expression, you embark on a journey of self-discovery that is both liberating and transformative.

In a world where voices are often stifled by self-doubt or the pressure to conform, embracing your unique expression becomes a radical act of faith. The words of Maya Angelou echo through time: ***"There is no greater agony than bearing an untold story inside you."*** By sharing your narrative, you not only free yourself from the weight of silence but also become a beacon of hope to those who may be struggling with their own hidden stories.

Your voice has the power to comfort the brokenhearted, to challenge injustice, and to uplift the weary. Each word, each melody, each creative spark is a testament to the work of God within you. As you dare to speak your truth, you invite others to experience the beauty of authenticity. You begin to understand that vulnerability is not a weakness but the very foundation of genuine connection. In moments of self-doubt, recall that your unique perspective is a gift meant to light up dark corners of the world.

Let your words be steeped in wisdom and compassion, reaching out to those who may be searching for meaning. Whether you are penning a heartfelt letter, sharing a prayer, or simply engaging in conversation, ***let your voice resonate with the echoes of divine truth***. It is in the honest articulation of your journey that you discover the true power of expression.

In embracing your voice, you also embrace the responsibility of being a storyteller of God's goodness. Your story, with all its trials and triumphs, becomes an instrument of healing and transformation. It is a call to be bold, to trust that what you have to share is not only needed but is essential for the edification of others. This is the essence of living authentically—allowing the light of your spirit to shine through every syllable, every gesture, every silent moment of connection.

Key Points:

- Your voice is a divine gift that carries the story of your life and God's work within you.
- Authentic expression fosters healing, connection, and inspiration.
- Embracing your narrative empowers you to share truth and hope with the world.
- Vulnerability in expression is the pathway to genuine, transformative relationships.

Reflection Questions:

1. What aspects of your story do you feel compelled to share with others?
2. How can you overcome the fears that keep your voice hidden?
3. In what ways can your unique expression serve as an inspiration to someone else?

Prayer to End the Chapter:

Heavenly Father, grant me the courage to embrace and express the unique voice You have given me. May my words and actions reflect Your truth and inspire hope in those who hear them. Help me to trust in the power of my story and to share it with grace and authenticity. Amen.

Chapter 23: The Strength of Community

Scripture:

"And let us consider how to stir up one another to love and good works." —Hebrews 10:24 **(ESV)**

Chapter Overview:

This chapter delves into the transformative power of community. It highlights how the fellowship of believers provides strength, support, and encouragement, creating an environment where every individual can thrive spiritually.

Chapter Content:

No one is meant to walk the journey of life alone. In the tapestry of faith, community is the thread that weaves us together, offering strength during times of trial and joy in moments of celebration. Within the embrace of a loving community, burdens are shared and the path ahead becomes clearer. Each person, with their unique story and gifts, contributes to a collective narrative that is rich in hope and encouragement.

Think of community as a sanctuary where you can lay down your fears and find comfort in shared experience. It is in the gentle exchange of stories, prayers, and acts of kindness that the wounds of isolation begin to heal. The challenges you face become more bearable when you have fellow travelers who are ready to offer a helping hand, a listening ear, or simply a word of affirmation. In this space, the love of God is not only experienced individually but multiplied among many.

There is beauty in the diversity of voices and experiences within a community. Each member adds a unique color to the canvas of collective faith, and together, you create a picture of resilience and unity. In times of joy, the laughter of friends lifts your spirit; in moments of sorrow, their compassion provides a soothing balm. The shared commitment to encouraging one another is a powerful force that propels the entire community forward.

As you actively participate in community life, you begin to see that every encounter is an opportunity to build bridges and sow seeds of hope. Whether it's through small group gatherings, service projects, or spontaneous acts of kindness, each interaction reaffirms that you are an integral part of a larger family—a family united not by geography or circumstance but by the love of God.

The strength of community lies in its ability to remind you that your struggles are not yours to bear alone. When you lift your eyes and see the faces of those who care, you find renewed hope and the courage to press on. Remember that even in the darkest seasons, the collective light of community can dispel loneliness and ignite a passion for life. In this fellowship, every challenge is met with prayer, every setback with support, and every victory is celebrated as a shared blessing.

Key Points:

- Community provides a supportive network that strengthens and uplifts every member.
- Shared experiences and mutual encouragement help alleviate the burdens of life.
- The diverse gifts of each individual contribute to the richness of collective faith.
- Active participation in community life fosters growth, unity, and resilience.

Reflection Questions:

1. How has being part of a community supported you during difficult times?
2. In what ways can you contribute to creating a more nurturing environment within your community?
3. What relationships in your life have most significantly reflected God's love and care?

Prayer to End the Chapter:

Lord, thank You for the gift of community. May I always cherish the bonds of fellowship and be a source of encouragement to those around me. Help me to actively build and nurture relationships that reflect Your love and bring hope to others. Amen.

Chapter 24: The Journey of Forgiveness

Scripture:

"Be kind to one another, tenderhearted, forgiving one another, as God in Christ forgave you." —Ephesians 4:32 **(ESV)**

Chapter Overview:

Forgiveness is a powerful act that liberates the soul. In this chapter, you are invited to journey through the process of letting go of past hurts and embracing a future filled with healing and renewal.

Chapter Content:

Forgiveness is not a single moment but a lifelong journey—a deliberate, sometimes difficult, decision to release the weight of resentment and anger. It is a process that requires both humility and strength, as you choose to let go of the past in order to step into the promise of a brighter future. When you forgive, you are not excusing the wrongs done to you; rather, you are reclaiming your peace and opening your heart to healing.

Every wound carries its own story, a history of pain that may have once felt insurmountable. Yet, in surrendering the desire for retribution, you find the courage to transform your sorrow into a testimony of grace. Reflect on the words of **Lewis B. Smedes**: ***"To forgive is to set a prisoner free and discover that the prisoner was you."*** In choosing forgiveness, you liberate yourself from the chains of past hurt and open the door to genuine transformation.

The path to forgiveness often begins with a deep sense of compassion—for yourself as much as for the one who hurt you. It is an invitation to see the humanity in every person, understanding that we are all flawed and in need of mercy. As you let go of bitterness, you make room for the healing power of God's love to fill every crevice of your heart. This act of releasing anger and pain is not a sign of weakness; rather, it is an affirmation of your strength and your commitment to live in freedom.

In the quiet moments of reflection, you may recall times when forgiveness has mended relationships and renewed hope. These memories serve as a reminder that every act of forgiveness, no matter how small, is a step toward a more peaceful and joyful life. Embrace the journey with patience and grace, knowing that each step forward brings you closer to the healing that only God can provide.

Forgiveness is a gift you give to yourself—a way of reclaiming your inner peace and stepping boldly into the future. It is a daily practice that transforms your spirit and paves the way for renewed relationships, both with others and with God. With every act of forgiveness, you move one step closer to the wholeness that is promised in His Word.

Key Points:

- Forgiveness is a deliberate choice that sets you free from the past.
- It is an act of strength that invites healing and restoration.
- Embracing forgiveness nurtures compassion and paves the way for new beginnings.
- Letting go of bitterness transforms your inner landscape and renews hope.

Reflection Questions:

1. What past hurt do you feel called to release through forgiveness?
2. How has forgiveness transformed your life in previous experiences?
3. What steps can you take today to begin the journey toward healing?

Prayer to End the Chapter:

Merciful God, grant me the strength and compassion to forgive those who have wronged me, and even to forgive myself. Help me to release the weight of past hurts and to embrace the healing power of

Your love. May forgiveness bring renewal to my heart and restore my spirit for a brighter tomorrow. Amen.

Chapter 25: Crafting a Life of Legacy

Scripture:

"For what does it profit a man to gain the whole world and forfeit his soul?" —Mark 8:36 **(ESV)**

Chapter Overview:

In this chapter, you are challenged to reflect on the lasting impact of your life. Legacy is defined not by material achievements but by the ways in which you invest in relationships, serve others, and live out values that echo into eternity.

Chapter Content:

Legacy is the imprint of your life—an enduring testimony of who you are and what you stand for. It is built one intentional act at a time, whether through a kind word, a selfless deed, or the pursuit of justice and love. When you consider the legacy you wish to leave behind, think beyond the fleeting accolades and consider the eternal influence of your actions.

Every decision, no matter how small, contributes to the narrative of your life. Your legacy is woven into the fabric of relationships, the impact you have on your community, and the values you uphold. It is a tapestry crafted with threads of compassion, integrity, and unwavering faith. Reflect on the words of Winston Churchill: ***"We***

make a living by what we get, but we make a life by what we give." This reminder calls you to invest in the lives around you, sowing seeds of hope and love that will continue to grow long after you are gone.

Crafting a life of legacy requires intentional living. It means being present in every moment, making choices that align with your deepest values, and striving to leave behind a world that is kinder, more just, and filled with love. When you commit to living in this way, you transform ordinary moments into extraordinary acts of service. Whether through mentoring, acts of kindness, or simply living authentically, your legacy is built day by day.

Consider the influence of those who have inspired you—their lives, marked by dedication and sacrifice, serve as blueprints for the legacy you might create. Their stories remind you that a life well-lived is not measured by the accumulation of wealth or power but by the enduring impact on the hearts of others. As you plan for your future, ask yourself: ***What story do I want my life to tell? How do I want to be remembered?***

Legacy is both a challenge and an opportunity—a call to invest deeply in the things that matter. It is an invitation to leave behind a world that reflects the transformative power of God's love, a world where each act of compassion creates a ripple that touches lives far beyond your own.

Key Points:

- Legacy is built through intentional, everyday acts of love and service.
- The impact of your life is measured by the values you uphold and the relationships you nurture.
- Investing in others creates a ripple effect that transcends time and place.
- A meaningful legacy is defined by its eternal influence, not by temporary accolades.

Reflection Questions:

1. What values do you wish to pass on to future generations?
2. How do your daily actions contribute to the legacy you are creating?
3. In what ways can you invest more deeply in the lives of those around you?

Prayer to End the Chapter:

Lord, help me to live each day with intention and purpose, crafting a legacy that honors You. May my actions be a testament to Your love and truth, leaving an enduring mark on the hearts of those I encounter. Guide me in building a legacy that reflects Your eternal grace. Amen.

Chapter 26: Walking in Divine Confidence

Scripture:

"So we can confidently say, 'The Lord is my helper; I will not fear; what can man do to me?'" —Hebrews 13:6 **(ESV)**

Chapter Overview:

This chapter challenges you to walk boldly, anchored in a confidence that comes not from self-reliance but from the unchanging strength of God. Divine confidence is portrayed as an inner assurance that empowers you to overcome fear and embrace your true identity.

Chapter Content:

True confidence is forged in the fire of divine truth—a confidence that emanates from the knowledge that you are cherished, empowered, and equipped by God. As you navigate the twists and turns of life, you learn that external validation is fleeting, but the assurance of God's presence is constant. When doubts arise and obstacles seem insurmountable, the inner conviction that ***"I am enough in Christ"*** becomes a steadfast anchor.

Reflect on the lives of biblical heroes who, despite overwhelming odds, stepped forward with unwavering resolve. Their confidence was not born of their own abilities but was a reflection of their deep trust in God's promises. In the same way, you are invited to embrace a bold, unshakable confidence—a walking declaration that your strength comes from a power far greater than your own. As you stand at the precipice of each new challenge, remember that every setback is a setup for divine breakthrough.

Empower yourself with the words of modern wisdom: *"Confidence is not about always having the right answer, but trusting that you have the right guide."* This guide, the eternal God, assures you that every step you take is divinely orchestrated. Even in the face of uncertainty, your identity as a beloved child of God becomes the foundation on which you build your life. Every trial, every victory, and every moment of doubt is an opportunity to lean into His strength, allowing His truth to dissolve your fears.

This chapter is a call to cast aside the shackles of self-doubt and to rise in the power of divine assurance. With each step forward, remind yourself that you are not defined by your failures, but by the promise that God is with you. In the quiet moments of reflection, let the truth of His Word wash over you, filling your spirit with a courage that no earthly circumstance can diminish. Step forward boldly, knowing that you are empowered by the Creator of the universe—a confidence that transforms obstacles into opportunities and fear into faith.

Key Points:

- Divine confidence stems from a deep trust in God's unfailing presence and promises.
- True strength is not self-generated but is a gift from God.
- Every challenge is an opportunity to exercise and reinforce your faith.
- Confidence rooted in divine truth overcomes fear and doubt.

Reflection Questions:

1. What fears have you encountered that have challenged your confidence?
2. How does knowing your identity in Christ influence your ability to face challenges?`
3. What practical steps can you take to cultivate a more confident spirit in God?

Prayer to End the Chapter:

Heavenly Father, instill in me a divine confidence that transcends fear and doubt. Help me to stand firm in the truth of who I am in You, trusting that every step is guided by Your loving hand. May Your strength be my foundation, and Your promises the light that leads me forward. Amen.

Chapter 27: Trusting God with the Unknown

Scripture:

"Trust in the Lord with all your heart, and do not lean on your own understanding." —Proverbs 3:5 (**ESV)**

Chapter Overview:

This chapter focuses on the challenge of facing the unknown with unwavering trust. It calls you to embrace uncertainty as a fertile ground for growth and divine intervention, reinforcing the idea that faith is most powerful when you step forward without all the answers.

Chapter Content:

There are times when the future appears shrouded in mystery, when the road ahead is unclear, and every step seems to lead into a fog of uncertainty. In these moments, the invitation is simple yet profound: trust in the Lord. Even when logic fails to provide comfort, your faith can become a beacon of light that guides you through the murkiness of doubt.

Consider the many biblical accounts of individuals who stepped into the unknown—Abraham leaving his homeland, Moses leading his people through the wilderness, and Peter stepping out of a boat onto turbulent waters. Their stories remind you that it is precisely in these moments of uncertainty that God's power is most evident. Trusting God with the unknown means relinquishing control and allowing divine wisdom to direct your path. It is an act of surrender that requires courage, patience, and a steadfast heart.

When you feel overwhelmed by the uncertainties of life, remember that each unanswered question is an opportunity to deepen your relationship with God. Rather than being paralyzed by fear, allow your trust in His goodness to propel you forward. Embrace the mystery with an open heart, knowing that every twist and turn is part of a larger, divine plan—a plan that is crafted with care and love beyond your understanding.

In times of uncertainty, let go of the need for immediate answers and rest in the assurance that God is working behind the scenes. His timing is perfect, and every delay is a precursor to a breakthrough. The challenges you face today are the very experiences that will shape you into a stronger, wiser, and more resilient individual tomorrow. Each moment spent in the unknown becomes a lesson in faith, an opportunity to witness the miraculous unfolding of God's plan in real time.

As you journey through periods of uncertainty, anchor yourself in prayer and reflection. Seek comfort in Scripture and allow the promises of God to fill your heart with peace. Trust that even when you cannot see the whole picture, His guidance is ever-present.

Embrace the unknown not as a void of fear, but as a canvas upon which God is painting the masterpiece of your life.

Key Points:

- Trusting God with the unknown is an invitation to embrace uncertainty with faith.
- Unanswered questions and unclear paths are opportunities for divine intervention.
- Biblical examples remind us that stepping into the unknown can lead to transformative breakthroughs.
- Surrendering control in uncertain times deepens your reliance on God's wisdom and timing.

Reflection Questions:

1. What uncertainties in your life currently challenge your ability to trust fully?
2. How have past experiences of the unknown strengthened your faith?
3. What practices can help you lean more on God's guidance during uncertain times?

Prayer to End the Chapter:

Lord, in moments when the future seems uncertain and the path unclear, help me to trust You wholeheartedly. Fill my heart with the courage to step forward, knowing that Your guidance is always with me. May I find peace in surrender and strength in the mystery of Your perfect plan. Amen.

Chapter 28: The Beauty of Brokenness

Scripture:

"The LORD is close to the brokenhearted and saves those who are crushed in spirit." —Psalm 34:18 **(NIV)**

Chapter Overview:

This chapter redefines brokenness as a space where healing and transformation take root. It shows how our vulnerabilities and wounds can become the very source of strength and a testament to the redemptive power of God's love.

Chapter Content:

Every fracture in your life, every moment of pain or loss, is not the end of your story but the beginning of a deeper healing process. Brokenness, while painful, holds a peculiar beauty—it is where raw honesty meets divine restoration. When you feel shattered by life's trials, know that this is precisely when God's healing touch is most evident. Rather than being defined by your wounds, you are invited to allow them to become the channels through which His grace flows abundantly.

Consider the transformative power of a shattered vessel. In its broken state, it can be mended with gold, creating a unique beauty that is far more precious than the original. Similarly, your moments of brokenness are opportunities for God to work wonders in your heart. As you navigate the pain, you begin to discover that what once hurt you can become a source of compassion, strength, and even inspiration for others. It is in our deepest wounds that the light of God's love can shine the brightest, revealing truths that no superficial strength ever could.

In the midst of sorrow, allow yourself to grieve, to feel, and ultimately, to be healed. ***Every tear, every sigh, is a step toward the wholeness that God promises***. This journey through brokenness is not one of weakness, but of profound resilience—a reminder that even in our most fragile moments, we are being remade into something new and beautiful.

Your brokenness invites you to release the burdens of shame and regret, replacing them with hope and renewal. It is an invitation to surrender the parts of yourself that have been weighed down by past hurts, and to allow God's restorative power to work its magic. In doing so, you not only reclaim your inner strength but also become a living testimony to the transformative nature of divine love.

Each scar you bear is a story of survival and a marker of God's faithfulness. Instead of hiding your wounds, consider them as symbols of a journey that has brought you closer to the heart of God. Embrace the beauty that emerges from the cracks, knowing that it is in these spaces that His light shines through most brilliantly.

Key Points:

- Brokenness is an opportunity for divine healing and transformation.
- Wounds, when surrendered to God, can become sources of strength and testimony.
- Embracing vulnerability leads to a deeper, more authentic experience of God's love.
- Every scar tells a story of resilience, redemption, and renewed hope.

Reflection Questions:

1. In what areas of your life do you feel most broken, and how might God be inviting you to heal?
2. How can you transform your vulnerabilities into sources of strength?
3. What practical steps can you take to allow God's restorative power to work in your wounds?

Prayer to End the Chapter:

Lord, I come before You with a heart that is bruised and in need of healing. Restore me, mend my brokenness, and fill the cracks with Your unending love. May my scars be a testimony to Your grace and a beacon of hope for others. Amen.

Chapter 29: Unshakable Faith

Scripture:

"For we live by faith, not by sight." —2 Corinthians 5:7 **(NIV)**

Chapter Overview:

This chapter calls you to cultivate a faith that stands firm regardless of life's turbulent circumstances. It emphasizes that true faith is not a passive state but an active commitment to trust in God even when all evidence seems to point to uncertainty.

Chapter Content:

Faith is a journey marked by both peaks and valleys—a steadfast trust that does not waver even when the way forward is obscured by doubt and fear. It is the quiet conviction in your heart that assures you of God's presence and His promises, regardless of what you see or understand at the moment. When storms arise and the world around you seems to crumble, that unshakable faith becomes your anchor, holding you fast to the truth that God is in control.

Reflect on the many moments in Scripture when faith triumphed over the visible chaos: the Israelites crossing the Red Sea, Peter stepping out of the boat onto stormy waters, or the apostle Paul enduring hardships with an unwavering trust in God's purpose. These stories are not just historical accounts—they are living testimonies that encourage you to press on, even when the path is uncertain. Every challenge you encounter is an opportunity to deepen your faith and to see firsthand that God's strength is made perfect in weakness.

Unshakable faith is forged in the crucible of life's adversities. It is a choice made each day—to believe in the unseen, to trust in divine promises even when circumstances suggest otherwise. As you journey through moments of doubt, remind yourself that faith is not about having all the answers but about holding fast to the One who does. Even when fear whispers that you are alone, let the truth of God's Word remind you that you are never abandoned.

Consider the wise words of **C.S. Lewis**: ***"Faith is the art of holding on to things your reason has once accepted, in spite of your changing moods."*** Let this truth be your guide as you navigate the complexities of life. Even in the darkest times, your faith is a light that cannot be extinguished—a light that reveals the steadfast nature of God's promises.

Every step taken in faith builds resilience. With each act of trust, you create a foundation that no storm can shake. The journey is not always easy, but the assurance that God is with you transforms every trial into an opportunity for growth. Embrace each challenge as a chance to reaffirm your commitment to walking by faith, knowing that even if you cannot see the full picture, His plan for you is unfolding perfectly.

Key Points:

- Unshakable faith is built on the promise of God's constant presence.
- Life's trials are opportunities to deepen and strengthen your trust in Him.
- Faith is an active choice that perseveres even in the absence of clear answers.
- The stories of biblical heroes serve as inspiration for overcoming doubt and fear.

Reflection Questions:

1. What recent challenges have tested your faith, and how did you respond?
2. In what ways can you build a stronger foundation of trust in God?
3. How does your understanding of faith change during times of uncertainty?

Prayer to End the Chapter:

Lord, strengthen my faith so that it may remain unshakable, even in the midst of life's storms. Help me to trust in Your unfailing promises and to walk boldly in the light of Your truth, regardless of what I cannot see. Amen.

Chapter 30: Embracing Change Gracefully

Scripture:

"He who was seated on the throne said, 'I am making everything new!" —Revelation 21:5 **(NIV)**

Chapter Overview:

This chapter examines change as an inevitable and essential part of life. It encourages you to welcome each transition as an opportunity for growth and transformation, trusting that every change is guided by God's loving hand.

Chapter Content:

Change is an ever-present companion on the journey of life—a force that reshapes our experiences, our relationships, and our very selves. While the prospect of change can sometimes evoke fear and uncertainty, it also holds the promise of renewal and transformation. God's declaration in Revelation reminds you that He is continuously at work, making all things new. ***This divine remodeling is not random; it is a deliberate process aimed at refining and perfecting the masterpiece of your life.***

As you encounter changes—whether gradual transitions or sudden shifts—recognize that each one carries the potential for deep personal growth. There is beauty in letting go of what no longer serves you, in releasing the old to welcome the new. Consider the metaphor of a tree shedding its leaves in autumn, only to bloom vibrantly in spring. Similarly, the changes in your life are part of a natural cycle of release, renewal, and rebirth. ***Embracing change means acknowledging that every ending is a precursor to a new beginning.***

In moments when change feels overwhelming, allow yourself the space to breathe and reflect. Take comfort in knowing that each transition is a step toward becoming the person God intends you to be. Instead of resisting change, invite it as a vital part of your journey—a chance to shed old habits, embrace fresh perspectives, and grow in ways you never imagined. Remember the wise words of Heraclitus: ***"The only constant in life is change."*** This truth, while sometimes challenging, is also liberating, for it means that nothing remains static, and there is always room for improvement and hope.

Let your heart be open to the unexpected opportunities that change may bring. Whether it is a new relationship, a different career path, or a shift in your personal outlook, each change is an invitation to explore the depth of God's creativity in your life. Trust that even in moments of uncertainty, God's plan is unfolding perfectly—every twist and turn is a part of a larger design that is both beautiful and purposeful.

Change, when embraced with grace, becomes a catalyst for personal transformation and spiritual renewal. It teaches you to let go of the past, to trust in the future, and to walk confidently into the unknown with a heart filled with hope and anticipation. Through each transformation, you are continually being shaped into a reflection of God's love and wisdom.

Key Points:

- Change is an inevitable part of life that leads to growth and renewal.
- Embracing change with faith transforms uncertainty into an opportunity for transformation.
- Each transition is part of God's deliberate process of refining and renewing your life.
- Letting go of the past creates space for new beginnings and deeper hope.

Reflection Questions:

1. What recent changes in your life have challenged you, and what have you learned from them?

2. How can you better embrace transitions as opportunities for growth?
3. What practices help you remain hopeful and trusting during times of change?

Prayer to End the Chapter:

Lord, help me to embrace change with a spirit of hope and trust. As I let go of the old, may I welcome the new with open arms, confident that Your hand is guiding every step of my transformation. Renew my heart and mind, and fill me with the courage to move forward gracefully. Amen.

Chapter 31: Awakening to Purpose

Scripture:

"For I know the plans I have for you, declares the Lord, plans for welfare and not for evil, to give you a future and a hope." — Jeremiah 29:11 **(ESV)**

Chapter Overview:

This chapter calls you to awaken to the purpose uniquely designed for your life. It invites you to listen intently for God's call and to align your daily actions with that divine direction, embracing every experience as a stepping stone toward your destiny.

Chapter Content:

Deep within the quiet of your soul, there lies an echo of a divine plan that is meant only for you. Awakening to your purpose is not an overnight epiphany but a gradual unveiling—a process of introspection, prayer, and courageous steps toward living authentically. Each moment, every triumph and trial, contributes to a mosaic that forms your destiny. When you begin to see your life through the lens of purpose, even the mundane transforms into the miraculous.

Consider the journey of a seed planted in the dark soil. At first, it seems dormant, hidden from the light. Yet, within that obscurity, a transformation is taking place—a metamorphosis that will soon break forth into vibrant life. In much the same way, your purpose is being nurtured quietly, even in the periods of waiting or uncertainty. Though you may not see the full picture right away, every experience, every challenge, is carefully orchestrated by a loving Creator.

To awaken to purpose, you must first be willing to listen—to the whispers of your heart, to the guidance of Scripture, and to the gentle nudges of the Spirit. It may mean stepping outside your comfort zone and embracing new opportunities, even when the outcome is uncertain. Purpose is not found in complacency but in the willingness to be molded by the hands of God. It requires you to let go of past expectations and to open your heart to the unexpected directions He may lead you.

Inspirational words from **Viktor Frankl** remind us that ***"life is never made unbearable by circumstances, but only by lack of meaning and purpose."*** In those moments when life feels heavy, seek the hidden meaning behind your experiences. ***Every setback has a lesson; every joy carries a message***. Trust that your life is not a series of random events but a carefully crafted narrative, with each chapter leading to the next.

Living with purpose means embracing the fullness of who you are meant to be. It means allowing your talents, passions, and experiences to converge into a powerful testimony of faith and hope. As you walk this path, you may find that your purpose not only brings clarity to your own life but also serves as a beacon for others who are searching for meaning. Your story, with its unique challenges and victories, has the power to inspire and uplift those around you.

Do not be discouraged if the path seems winding or the destination distant. Every step you take in faith, even if small or seemingly insignificant, contributes to the unfolding of your destiny. Embrace each day as a new opportunity to learn, grow, and move closer to the purpose that God has lovingly prepared for you.

Key Points:

- Your purpose is a unique design crafted by God, revealed through life's experiences.
- Awakening to purpose involves listening to your heart, Scripture, and the Spirit's guidance.
- Every challenge and joy plays a role in the unfolding narrative of your destiny.
- Living purposefully transforms your life into a testimony of faith and hope.

Reflection Questions:

1. What moments in your life have hinted at a deeper purpose?
2. How can you better listen for God's guidance in your daily routine?
3. What steps can you take to align your actions with the calling you sense within you?

Prayer to End the Chapter:

Lord, open my heart and mind to the purpose You have set before me. Help me to listen intently to Your guidance and to trust in the path You are laying out. May I embrace each moment as an opportunity to grow into the person You created me to be, and may my life become a testament to Your loving plan. Amen.

Chapter 32: Cultivating Inner Peace

Scripture:

"And the peace of God, which surpasses all understanding, will guard your hearts and your minds in Christ Jesus." —Philippians 4:7 **(ESV)**

Chapter Overview:

This chapter focuses on cultivating a deep, abiding inner peace that can sustain you amid life's storms. It explores the practices of prayer, mindfulness, and surrender as pathways to a tranquil spirit anchored in God's love.

Chapter Content:

In a world bustling with noise and constant demands, inner peace is a sanctuary that resides within—a quiet refuge untouched by the chaos of daily life. Cultivating this peace is not about escaping reality but about finding a stable ground in the midst of uncertainty. It is an intentional practice of surrendering your anxieties to a God who is bigger than every worry that may cloud your mind.

Inner peace begins with the simple act of pausing. In the midst of a busy day, take a few moments to step away from the clamor and reconnect with your Creator. Whether through silent meditation, reflective prayer, or simply breathing deeply while focusing on

God's promises, these practices nurture a sense of calm that flows into every part of your being.

Think of inner peace as the still waters of a hidden lake—quiet, deep, and full of life. The surface may ripple when disturbed, but beneath, there remains a constant, unchanging tranquility. In the same way, your soul can remain undisturbed by the fleeting troubles of the world if you anchor it in the truth of God's word. The promise of Philippians assures you that ***His peace is not bound by circumstances; it is a divine gift that transcends human understanding.***

Drawing on the wisdom of spiritual teachers, you may recall that true peace often comes when you let go. It is in releasing the grip on control, on the need to have all the answers, that you discover the freedom to simply be. When you surrender your burdens, you allow the light of God's love to penetrate the darkest corners of your heart. This surrender is not an act of defeat but a courageous decision to trust that God's plan is perfect.

Consider the impact of daily gratitude on your inner peace. When you consciously choose to recognize the blessings in your life—no matter how small—you shift your focus from scarcity to abundance. Gratitude is a powerful antidote to worry; it opens your eyes to the goodness that surrounds you and reinforces your trust in God's providence.

In moments when anxiety creeps in, remind yourself of the timeless truth: God's peace is available to you in every situation. It is a steady reminder that, regardless of the external storms, the heart anchored in God remains unshaken. As you cultivate this inner peace, you will find that it radiates outward, influencing your interactions and the way you navigate the world.

Key Points:

- Inner peace is a divine gift that transcends external circumstances.
- Practices such as prayer, meditation, and gratitude nurture a tranquil spirit.
- Surrendering control is essential to experiencing true peace.
- An anchored heart in God reflects and radiates peace to those around you.

Reflection Questions:

1. What practices help you cultivate inner peace during stressful times?
2. How does gratitude shift your perspective in moments of anxiety?
3. In what ways can you create more moments of stillness in your daily life?

Prayer to End the Chapter:

Lord, fill my heart with the peace that only You can give. Help me to release my worries and to rest in the assurance of Your love. May Your tranquility guard my mind and spirit, guiding me to live each day in calm and confident trust. Amen.

Chapter 33: Embracing New Beginnings

Scripture:

"Therefore, if anyone is in Christ, the new creation has come: The old has gone, the new is here!" —2 Corinthians 5:17 **(NIV)**

Chapter Overview:

This chapter celebrates the transformative power of new beginnings. It encourages you to let go of past burdens and to step forward into fresh opportunities, trusting that every ending paves the way for a vibrant new start.

Chapter Content:

Every new beginning is a fresh canvas—an invitation to rewrite the story of your life with hope, courage, and faith. The promise of renewal in Christ means that no matter what has transpired, there is always an opportunity to start anew. In this light, new beginnings are not just changes; they are the blossoming of a life continuously reformed by God's grace.

Think of a sunrise after a long, dark night. The gradual light creeping over the horizon signifies that the darkness has passed and a new day is dawning. Similarly, each new beginning in your life carries the promise of light, hope, and transformation. It is a time to leave behind what no longer serves you and to embrace the infinite possibilities that lie ahead.

Embracing new beginnings requires a willingness to let go. Often, the hardest part of moving forward is releasing the weight of past mistakes, regrets, or losses. Yet, it is in that act of surrender that you make room for something greater. When you choose to leave behind the old, you create space for the divine to work wonders in your life. This process is not about erasing memories but about transforming them into lessons that guide you toward a better future.

Consider the wise words of **Rumi**: ***"Yesterday I was clever, so I wanted to change the world. Today I am wise, so I am changing myself."*** In this transformation, you come to understand that the journey of change starts within. Every decision to embrace the new—be it a new relationship, a fresh career path, or a renewed outlook on life—becomes an act of faith, a declaration that you are ready for God's transformative work.

As you step into new beginnings, cultivate an attitude of curiosity and openness. Let go of the fear of the unknown, and instead see it as a realm of infinite possibility. Each moment is a chance to reinvent yourself, to grow, and to align more closely with the purpose God has laid out for you. With every step forward, you are rewriting your story—one filled with hope, resilience, and divine promise.

Remember that new beginnings are also opportunities to heal. They allow you to mend broken parts of your past and to integrate them into a narrative of redemption and renewal. The journey may be challenging at times, but the assurance of God's constant presence makes every step worth taking.

Key Points:

- New beginnings are transformative opportunities for growth and renewal.
- Letting go of the past is essential to embrace the future with hope.
- Each fresh start is a testament to God's unending grace and promise.
- A new beginning invites you to reinvent yourself and align more closely with your divine purpose.

Reflection Questions:

1. What past experiences are you ready to leave behind in order to embrace a new beginning?
2. How can you cultivate a mindset that welcomes change and renewal?
3. What new opportunities are emerging in your life right now?

Prayer to End the Chapter:

Lord, thank You for the gift of new beginnings. Help me to let go of the past and to step boldly into the future with hope and trust. May Your grace renew my spirit, and may each new day be a testament to Your transformative love. Amen.

Chapter 34: Nurturing Resilience

Scripture:

"Not only that, but we rejoice in our sufferings, knowing that suffering produces endurance." —Romans 5:3 **(ESV)**

Chapter Overview:

This chapter explores the concept of resilience as a vital strength formed in the crucible of life's challenges. It invites you to view each hardship as an opportunity for growth and to nurture the endurance that shapes your character.

Chapter Content:

Resilience is not merely about bouncing back—it is about growing stronger with each setback. Life's trials are inevitable, yet it is how you respond to these challenges that defines your strength. Resilience is forged in the fires of adversity, where the pressure of difficult circumstances molds you into a person of enduring character and hope.

Imagine a tree bending in the wind. The storms may bend its branches, but they do not break its roots. Your resilience is much like these deep roots, anchoring you firmly even when the winds of hardship blow fiercely. Every challenge you face, whether a personal loss, a professional setback, or emotional turmoil, carries within it the seed of renewal. Through these trials, you learn to adapt, to persevere, and ultimately, to thrive.

In cultivating resilience, you begin to see setbacks not as failures but as valuable lessons. Each obstacle becomes an opportunity to refine your character, to develop a deeper understanding of your inner strength, and to lean more fully on the support of God's enduring love. ***The process of building resilience often involves embracing vulnerability and acknowledging that you need help along the way.*** It is in those moments of honest reflection that you discover your true capacity to overcome.

Resilience is also nurtured through the power of community. When you share your struggles and triumphs with others, you create a network of support that reinforces your inner strength. Whether through the counsel of a trusted friend, the wisdom of a mentor, or the encouragement of a prayer group, the collective support you receive can bolster your resolve to keep moving forward.

The journey of resilience is a continuous one—a series of small victories that add up over time. Celebrate each moment of perseverance, for they are stepping stones toward a life defined not by the absence of pain but by the strength to rise above it. Remember that every challenge overcome builds a reservoir of courage that you can draw upon in the future.

Reflect on the words of **Nelson Mandela**: ***"Do not judge me by my success, judge me by how many times I fell down and got back up again."*** Let this truth inspire you to see every fall as an opportunity to stand taller, to learn, and to grow. Resilience transforms the trials of today into the triumphs of tomorrow, and it is in this process that you truly discover the depth of God's sustaining power.

Key Points:

- Resilience is the strength that emerges from facing and overcoming adversity.
- Each challenge is an opportunity to build endurance and deepen your character.
- Community support and vulnerability are essential in nurturing resilience.
- Embracing setbacks as lessons paves the way for future triumphs.

Reflection Questions:

1. What recent challenges have strengthened your resilience?
2. How do you view setbacks—as failures or opportunities for growth?
3. In what ways can you lean on community and faith to build a stronger foundation?

Prayer to End the Chapter:

Lord, grant me the strength to rise above every challenge. Help me to see each setback as a chance to grow and to build resilience through Your unwavering love. May I find courage in every trial and trust that You are shaping me into a vessel of hope and endurance. Amen.

Chapter 35: The Light of Hope

Scripture:

"For I know the plans I have for you, declares the Lord, plans to prosper you and not to harm you, plans to give you hope and a future." —Jeremiah 29:11 **(ESV)**

Chapter Overview:

In this chapter, hope is cast as the guiding light that dispels darkness. It encourages you to hold fast to God's promises even when circumstances seem bleak, illuminating your path with the assurance of a better tomorrow.

Chapter Content:

Hope is a radiant light that persists even in the darkest of times. It is not a fleeting emotion but a steadfast assurance rooted in the promises of God. When life presents its shadows—moments of despair, loss, and uncertainty—hope becomes the beacon that guides you forward. It is the belief that no matter how heavy the burden, there is a brighter future waiting just beyond the horizon.

The promise in Jeremiah reminds you that God's plans are designed for your good, for a future filled with hope. This divine assurance is a powerful antidote to the despair that can sometimes overwhelm the human spirit. ***When you anchor your heart in hope, you invite***

a renewal of strength and the courage to face life's challenges head-on.

Imagine walking through a long, dark tunnel and seeing the first hints of light at its end. That light symbolizes hope—a promise that the journey will eventually lead to a place of comfort and joy. Holding on to hope means trusting in the process, even when the road is long and the obstacles are many. It requires you to look beyond the present hardships and to envision a future where every tear is wiped away and every sorrow is replaced with joy.

Hope is nurtured by the small, everyday miracles that often go unnoticed—the kindness of a stranger, the beauty of nature, a word of encouragement, or a quiet moment of reflection. These moments remind you that God is present in every detail of life, working behind the scenes to bring forth His promises. Even when the path is uncertain, each step taken in faith is a testament to the enduring light of hope.

To cultivate hope, you must also practice gratitude. By acknowledging the blessings in your life, you create a foundation upon which hope can flourish. Gratitude shifts your focus from what is missing to what is abundantly present, reinforcing the truth that God's love is constant and His plans are good.

In times when hope seems distant, remember the words of **Emily Dickinson:** ***"Hope is the thing with feathers that perches in the soul and sings the tune without the words, and never stops at all."*** Let this imagery inspire you to nurture the small, persistent flame of hope within you. Each act of faith, each moment of perseverance, fuels that light and propels you toward a future filled with promise.

Key Points:

- Hope is a steadfast light that endures even in darkness.
- God's promises ensure a future filled with hope and renewal.
- Everyday blessings and gratitude nurture a resilient spirit of hope.
- Holding on to hope transforms despair into the anticipation of brighter days.

Reflection Questions:

1. What are the small signs of hope you notice in your everyday life?
2. How can you cultivate a mindset that focuses on the promises of God?
3. In what ways does hope sustain you during difficult times?

Prayer to End the Chapter:

Lord, fill my heart with the light of hope that only You can provide. Help me to trust in Your promises and to see beyond the present darkness into the future You have prepared. May Your hope be my constant companion and guide me toward a life filled with joy and renewal. Amen.

Chapter 36: Walking with Wisdom

Scripture:

"If any of you lacks wisdom, let him ask God, who gives generously to all without reproach." —James 1:5 **(ESV)**

Chapter Overview:

This chapter invites you to seek and walk in divine wisdom. It emphasizes that true understanding comes from a humble reliance on God's guidance and encourages you to approach life's decisions with a spirit of discernment and openness.

Chapter Content:

Wisdom is more than knowledge—it is the ability to apply truth in every aspect of life. In a world brimming with conflicting voices and rapid change, walking with wisdom means turning to the One who is the source of all understanding. It is an invitation to pause, reflect, and seek guidance from God before making decisions, both big and small.

When faced with life's myriad choices, wisdom becomes your compass. It directs you not toward a path of ease, but toward one of growth and righteousness. Every decision made in the light of divine wisdom carries the assurance that you are aligned with God's perfect plan. Rather than relying solely on human reasoning, which can be clouded by fear and bias, wisdom calls you to a higher standard—a standard set by the Creator of all things.

Imagine wisdom as a wellspring that nourishes your soul. Each time you seek counsel through prayer, study Scripture, or listen to the wise counsel of others, you draw closer to the heart of God. This inner reservoir of wisdom becomes a source of strength and clarity, enabling you to navigate even the most challenging circumstances with grace. It is a light that shines in the darkness, illuminating the path forward with truth and understanding.

There is a humility inherent in the pursuit of wisdom. It requires acknowledging that you do not have all the answers and that true insight comes from surrendering your own preconceived notions. As you open yourself to God's guidance, you begin to see the interconnectedness of all things—each decision, each encounter, and each lesson interwoven into the fabric of your life's journey.

Practical steps to walk in wisdom include regular prayer, meditation on God's Word, and seeking counsel from trusted mentors. Each of these practices not only enriches your understanding but also deepens your relationship with the Source of all truth. With every decision made in humility and trust, you cultivate a heart that is both discerning and compassionate—a heart that reflects the wisdom of God in every thought and action.

The pursuit of wisdom is a lifelong journey. It is not achieved in a single moment but is built gradually, one insight at a time. As you continue to seek wisdom, remember that every experience—whether triumphant or challenging—is an opportunity to learn and grow. ***Embrace the journey with patience, knowing that God gives generously to all who ask***.

Key Points:

- Walking with wisdom involves seeking God's guidance in every decision.
- True wisdom is rooted in humility, reflection, and a reliance on divine truth.
- Regular prayer, study, and counsel are essential practices for cultivating wisdom.
- Wisdom transforms your perspective, leading to decisions that honor God's plan.

Reflection Questions:

1. In what areas of your life do you need to seek more wisdom?
2. How can you incorporate practices like prayer and reflection into your daily routine?
3. What experiences have taught you valuable lessons that now inform your decisions?

Prayer to End the Chapter:

Heavenly Father, grant me the wisdom that comes from Your boundless love and truth. Help me to seek Your guidance in every decision and to walk humbly in the light of Your understanding. May Your wisdom shape my heart and lead me on the path of righteousness. Amen.

Chapter 37: Restoring Joy

Scripture:

"You make known to me the path of life; in your presence there is fullness of joy." —Psalm 16:11 **(ESV)**

Chapter Overview:

This chapter focuses on the restorative power of joy, encouraging you to reconnect with the simple, profound happiness that comes from dwelling in God's presence. It explores how joy can be restored even in the midst of adversity.

Chapter Content:

Joy is a deep, abiding delight that transcends momentary happiness. It is the inner glow that persists even when external circumstances seem bleak. ***Restoring joy in your life is a conscious decision to embrace God's presence, finding beauty and hope in every moment, no matter how challenging***.

Life's difficulties can often overshadow the light of joy, leaving your heart heavy with sorrow. Yet, amid the trials, there is an invitation to rediscover that joy—a joy that is not dependent on circumstances but rooted in the eternal love of God. In moments of quiet reflection, allow yourself to be reminded that the fullness of joy is found in the presence of the Lord. His love has the power to heal wounds, to lift burdens, and to bring a renewed sense of purpose and happiness.

To restore joy, begin by cultivating a spirit of gratitude.

When you intentionally focus on the blessings in your life—whether big or small—you create a fertile ground for joy to flourish. It might be as simple as appreciating a kind gesture from a friend, the beauty of a sunset, or the comforting words of Scripture. Each of these moments serves as a reminder that God's goodness is ever-present, even when life seems challenging.

Moreover, restoring joy often involves surrendering to the present moment. Allow yourself to fully experience the here and now without being burdened by regrets of the past or fears of the future. Embrace the simplicity of living in the moment, where joy can be found in the quiet assurance that God is with you. The psalmist declares that in ***God's presence there is fullness of joy***—an invitation to experience a peace that surpasses all understanding.

Additionally, remember that ***joy is contagious***. When you cultivate joy within your heart, it radiates outward, touching the lives of those around you. Acts of kindness, a smile, or a sincere word of encouragement can spread joy and uplift others who may be struggling. In this way, the restoration of joy is not a solitary pursuit but a communal celebration of God's goodness.

Reflect on the transformative power of joy in your own life. ***Recall times when, despite hardships, a moment of divine intervention or a loving gesture brought light into your darkness.*** These memories are powerful reminders that joy is not fleeting but can be a constant companion when nurtured by faith. Allow these experiences to strengthen your resolve to seek and restore joy every day.

Key Points:

- Joy is an enduring state that transcends temporary happiness.
- Restoring joy involves gratitude, presence, and a deep connection with God.
- Experiencing joy can transform your outlook and positively impact those around you.
- Even in adversity, God's presence brings a fullness of joy that is both healing and uplifting.

Reflection Questions:

1. What small moments in your life have brought you unexpected joy?
2. How can you cultivate gratitude to help restore a sense of joy?
3. In what ways can you share the joy you experience with others?

Prayer to End the Chapter:

Lord, restore the joy that only You can provide. Fill my heart with Your love and help me to live each day with a grateful spirit, mindful of the blessings that surround me. May Your presence be the wellspring of everlasting joy in my life, and may I share that light with all whom I encounter. Amen.

Chapter 38: Embracing Divine Timing

Scripture:

"For everything there is a season, and a time for every activity under the heavens." —Ecclesiastes 3:1 **(NIV)**

Chapter Overview:

This chapter emphasizes the importance of trusting in God's perfect timing. It reassures you that every delay, every pause, and every season of waiting has a divine purpose and is an integral part of your journey toward fulfillment.

Chapter Content:

Life is a series of seasons, each marked by its own challenges and triumphs. ***Divine timing teaches you that every moment has its purpose***—even those that seem to be filled with waiting or delay. When plans do not unfold as quickly as you might hope, it is not a sign of abandonment but an opportunity for growth and preparation. God's timing, though sometimes mysterious, is always perfect, and every pause is a prelude to a breakthrough.

Consider the natural rhythms of life—the changing of the seasons, the ebb and flow of tides, and the cycles of day and night. Just as nature operates in perfect time, so does your life, under the guidance of a loving Creator. Each season, whether one of abundance or scarcity, joy or sorrow, contributes to the tapestry of your existence. It is in these cycles that you learn, evolve, and ultimately become more aligned with God's plan for your life.

When you find yourself in a season of waiting, resist the urge to rush or force outcomes. Instead, use this time to reflect, to prepare, and to trust that God is working behind the scenes. It is in the quiet intervals that He refines your character, strengthens your faith, and equips you for the next phase of your journey. ***The delays you experience are not denials***—they are divinely orchestrated pauses designed to prepare you for what is to come.

Allow yourself to embrace the beauty of divine timing by cultivating patience and faith. Surrender your plans and expectations, and open your heart to the possibilities that arise in the stillness. Trust that every setback is setting the stage for a greater comeback and that every unanswered prayer is a call to deeper reliance on God's wisdom. In time, what once seemed like obstacles will reveal themselves as essential stepping stones toward your destiny.

Reflect on past experiences where waiting led to unexpected blessings. These memories serve as a testament to the truth that God's timing is always perfect. Let them remind you that even when the road ahead is uncertain, a loving hand is guiding you toward a future filled with promise. Each moment of waiting is a lesson in trust and an invitation to grow in patience and perseverance.

Key Points:

- Divine timing is an integral part of your journey, shaping you for future blessings.
- Every season, even those marked by waiting, has a purpose in God's perfect plan.
- Patience and trust are essential in embracing the rhythms of life.
- Reflecting on past experiences can strengthen your faith in God's timing.

Reflection Questions:

1. What current delays in your life might actually be preparing you for something greater?
2. How can you practice patience and trust during seasons of waiting?
3. What past experiences remind you that God's timing is perfect?

Prayer to End the Chapter:

Lord, help me to trust in Your perfect timing. In the seasons of waiting, grant me patience and the strength to see Your hand at work in every detail of my life. May I rest in the assurance that every pause is purposeful and that You are preparing me for a future filled with hope and promise. Amen.

Chapter 39: Living Out Your Calling

Scripture:

"For we are his workmanship, created in Christ Jesus for good works, which God prepared beforehand, that we should walk in them." —Ephesians 2:10 **(ESV)**

Chapter Overview:

This chapter invites you to step boldly into the calling that God has placed on your life. It emphasizes that every talent, passion, and experience has been designed for a unique purpose, and that living out your calling is both an act of faith and a service to others.

Chapter Content:

Your calling is a tapestry of divine appointments, carefully woven by God's loving hands. It is not merely a job or a title, but a dynamic, living expression of who you are meant to be. To live out your calling, you must first recognize that every aspect of your life—every success, every failure, every joy, and every trial—is a brushstroke in the masterpiece of your destiny.

The journey toward fulfilling your calling begins with a deep, introspective awareness of your gifts and passions. ***What are the***

talents that set your soul on fire? What experiences have shaped your understanding of the world? As you explore these questions, you discover that your calling is not confined to a single moment or career—it is a continuous process of growth, learning, and service. It is the natural outpouring of a life lived in alignment with God's purpose.

Living out your calling requires courage.

It means stepping beyond the familiar and embracing the uncertainty of a path that is uniquely yours. There will be challenges along the way—moments of doubt, setbacks, and obstacles that test your resolve. Yet, it is in overcoming these challenges that your calling is fully realized. Each obstacle becomes an opportunity to demonstrate faith, perseverance, and the power of God working through you.

The apostle Paul reminds you that ***you are God's workmanship***, crafted with care and intended for good works. This truth is both empowering and liberating. It means that your life has intrinsic value, and that every act of service, every kind word, every step of courage is a reflection of God's love. Your calling is not just about personal fulfillment; it is a light that shines forth to guide and inspire others.

As you walk this path, remain open to the ways in which God continually refines and directs your steps. Seek wisdom in prayer, listen intently to the whispers of your heart, and be willing to adapt as your understanding of your calling deepens. The journey is not always linear, but every twist and turn brings you closer to the truth of who you are meant to be.

Your calling is a beacon of hope—not only for you but for those around you. ***When you live authentically and courageously, you create a ripple effect that encourages others to pursue their own divine purposes.*** The impact of living out your calling transcends the individual; it transforms communities, uplifts families, and leaves a lasting legacy of faith and love.

Key Points:

- Your calling is a unique expression of God's purpose, woven through every aspect of your life.
- Recognizing and living out your calling is a continuous journey of growth, service, and courage.
- Challenges along the way are opportunities to strengthen your faith and fulfill your destiny.
- Embracing your calling not only transforms your life but also inspires others.

Reflection Questions:

1. What gifts and passions do you believe are part of your calling?

2. How can you overcome obstacles that may be hindering you from fully stepping into your purpose?
3. In what ways can your life serve as an inspiration for others to seek their own divine calling?

Prayer to End the Chapter:

Lord, reveal to me the unique calling You have placed upon my life. Empower me to step boldly into the purpose You have designed, and help me to use my gifts to serve and inspire others. May my life be a living testament to Your love, and may I fulfill the destiny You have lovingly prepared for me. Amen.

Chapter 40: Stepping into Destiny Fulfilled

Scripture:

"For I know the plans I have for you, declares the Lord, plans for welfare and not for evil, to give you a future and a hope." — Jeremiah 29:11 **(ESV)**

Chapter Overview:

In this concluding chapter, you are invited to step fully into the destiny that God has prepared. It is a call to live with confidence, passion, and purpose—recognizing that every part of your journey has led you to this moment of fulfillment.

Chapter Content:

Destiny is not a distant dream but a present reality waiting to be claimed. Every experience, every lesson, and every trial has been a thread in the rich tapestry of your life—each one preparing you for this very moment. As you stand on the threshold of your destiny, reflect on the journey that has brought you here. The moments of doubt, the victories, the setbacks, and the breakthroughs have all converged to form a unique path that is unmistakably your own.

Stepping into your destiny means embracing the fullness of who you are meant to be. It is an act of bold faith—a declaration that you are ready to walk in the light of God's promises and to live out the purpose for which you were created. This is not a call to complacency but to action; it is an invitation to engage passionately with the world, using the talents and experiences God has given you to make a lasting impact.

Imagine your life as a story written by the hand of the Divine. Every chapter has led to this culminating moment—a time when you are empowered to step forward with clarity and conviction. The challenges you encountered were not punishments, but necessary preparations for the triumphs ahead. In this moment, you see that each struggle has refined your character, and every setback has paved the way for breakthroughs.

Now, as you stand on the brink of a new era, embrace the confidence that comes from knowing your life is guided by a loving and purposeful God. Every step you take from this point forward is part of a grand design—one that is infused with hope, promise, and the assurance of divine favor. Your destiny is a tapestry of all that you have been, all that you are, and all that you are yet to become.

Living out your destiny means being a beacon of light in a world that is often overshadowed by doubt and despair. It is about sharing your story, inspiring others to trust in their own journey, and using your unique gifts to bring about positive change. With each step, you affirm that your past does not define you, but rather, it propels you toward a future filled with potential and purpose.

As you step into destiny fulfilled, let your heart be filled with gratitude for the journey thus far. Celebrate the small victories and learn from the challenges, knowing that every moment has been a stepping stone toward this divine appointment. Embrace the future with an open heart, trusting that God's plan for you is both magnificent and unyielding.

Key Points:

- Destiny is the culmination of every experience, each preparing you for this moment.
- Stepping into destiny requires bold faith, active engagement, and a clear vision of God's promises.
- Your life's journey, with all its challenges and triumphs, serves as a testament to divine purpose.
- Living out your destiny means inspiring others and making a lasting impact on the world.

Reflection Questions:

1. How does your life's journey reflect the destiny God has prepared for you?

2. What steps can you take today to embrace your future with confidence and purpose?
3. In what ways can you use your unique story to inspire others to trust in their own journey?

Prayer to End the Chapter:

Lord, thank You for the journey that has led me to this moment of destiny. Empower me to step forward with boldness and faith, fully embracing the purpose You have prepared for my life. May I be a light that inspires others, and may every action I take be a testament to Your unwavering love and guidance. Amen.

Chapter 41: Access Comes with Alignment

Scripture:

"Commit to the Lord whatever you do, and He will establish your plans." —Proverbs 16:3 **(NIV)**

Chapter Overview:

This chapter reveals how access is not just about opportunity—it's about alignment. When your heart, habits, and mindset align with God's will, the right doors open, and the right timing follows.

Chapter Content:

Many people chase access. But in the kingdom of God, access chases alignment.

You don't have to manipulate your way into opportunity or force your way through doors. When your spirit, schedule, and purpose align with what God has called you to do, the access follows naturally.

Alignment is about posture before positioning.

You can't expect divine promotion if you're misaligned with divine priorities. God doesn't open doors based on our ambition—He opens them based on our submission.

This is where many of us get stuck. We want access without accountability. We want favor without obedience. We want breakthrough without surrender.

But access comes with alignment.

Alignment means letting go of what you want if it contradicts what God wants. It means being honest about your motives, open to correction, and willing to follow—even when the road curves differently than you expected.

The more aligned you are with God's will, the more at peace you are when something doesn't go your way—because you know if it didn't open, it wasn't for you. And if it ***is*** for you, nothing can keep it from you.

Alignment begins in your heart. When your desire is to please God more than to promote yourself, you begin walking in authority rather than anxiety. Your movements become intentional. Your decisions become prayerful. Your plans become God-led rather than ego-driven.

True alignment produces spiritual confidence. You stop striving. You start trusting. You walk with assurance. You speak with clarity. You wait without fear.

Alignment also creates room for acceleration. When your life is in sync with God's direction, what once took years may only take months. He redeems time for those who trust Him with it.

God honors alignment because it reflects humility and maturity. And it's in that place of humility that God can trust you with greater responsibility.

You don't need to force a door to open. You just need to be in the right position when God says, **"Now."**

So today, check your alignment. **Does your heart match His will? Does your vision reflect His purpose?** Are your plans built on your faith or your flesh?

Because the door you're praying for may already be swinging open—it's just waiting on you to get in position.

Key Points:

- Access is tied to alignment, not ambition.

- God opens doors for those positioned in surrender, not striving.
- Alignment produces clarity, confidence, and peace.
- Accelerated progress follows divine alignment.
- God trusts the aligned heart with greater doors.

Reflection Questions:

1. Are there areas in your life that feel out of alignment with God's will?
2. What habits or attitudes might be hindering your access?
3. How can you realign your daily choices with your faith?
4. What does spiritual alignment look like in your current season?
5. Are you pursuing God's plan or your personal agenda?
6. What steps can you take this week to move closer to divine alignment?

Prayer to End the Chapter:

God, align my heart with Yours. Strip away every motive, plan, or path that doesn't honor You. Help me to submit rather than strive, to trust rather than manipulate. I want the kind of access that comes from being in position—not from pushing for position. Lead me into Your will. Align my steps with Your Spirit. And when the moment comes, may I walk boldly into what You've prepared for me—fully aligned and fully surrendered.

Amen.

Chapter 42: Unexpected Keys

Scripture:

"I will give you the keys of the kingdom of heaven; whatever you bind on earth will be bound in heaven, and whatever you loose on earth will be loosed in heaven." —Matthew 16:19 **(NIV)**

Chapter Overview:

In this chapter, we discover that sometimes the access we're praying for won't come through the door we expected. God often places keys in our lives in unexpected places, people, and moments. The goal is to help readers recognize and embrace the unconventional ways God provides access.

Chapter Content:

We have a mental picture of how things are supposed to go. We expect the opportunity to come from a particular source, in a certain form, wrapped in clarity and timing that makes sense.

But God doesn't always hand you keys the way you imagined. Sometimes He hides them in unexpected places—obscure assignments, unlikely relationships, or low places that require humility.

Jesus handed Peter the **"keys of the kingdom,"** not after Peter got everything right, but after he recognized who Jesus truly was. Revelation brought the key—not perfection.

God will often use things that seem insignificant to unlock doors you didn't even know were there. That job you took out of necessity? That one connection that felt random? That conversation that didn't seem that deep at the time? They were all keys—quiet, holy moments of access.

Sometimes the key is found in serving where you're not celebrated. Sometimes it's in forgiving someone who hurt you. Other times, it's in saying yes to something that feels small but is actually connected to your big.

We must be careful not to dismiss the unlikely just because it doesn't look like destiny. David's key to the palace came through playing a harp. Joseph's key came through interpreting dreams in a prison. Ruth's access came through gleaning in a field.

The path to access isn't always glamorous—but it's always strategic.

God uses the unexpected to stretch your faith. To shift your perspective. To see if you'll trust the process when the packaging doesn't match the promise.

The keys are not always shiny. They don't always come with applause. But they open doors no man can shut. And when you find them—when you steward them well—you step into places you were born to walk through.

Often, the key looks like obedience in the quiet. Like helping someone when no one is watching. Like showing up to serve when you're not being acknowledged. These hidden moments build spiritual muscle and prepare you for what's coming.

There's power in being faithful in obscurity. There's power in saying yes when it doesn't make sense. There's power in trusting that God wastes nothing—not even the small steps that seem to go unnoticed.

So today, look again. Look at the assignments you've labeled ***"temporary."*** Look at the people you've overlooked. Look at the opportunities you thought were too small. That might just be where your key is waiting.

And when you find that key—hold it with gratitude. It's not just about getting access. It's about what you learned while you waited for it. It's about who you became while you were searching.

Because sometimes, the most important thing the key opens isn't the door—it's your perspective.

Key Points:

- God often hides keys in unexpected places and people.
- Revelation, not perfection, positions you for access.
- Small acts of obedience often unlock great doors.
- Don't overlook low places—they often hold high calling.
- What feels like "just a step" may be the start of everything.
- The process of finding the key is often more transformative than the door itself.

Reflection Questions:

1. Have you missed a potential key by assuming it was too small or insignificant?
2. What **"random"** connections or moments in your life may have been strategic?
3. How can you begin to view current opportunities with renewed spiritual vision?

4. Is there an area where God is asking you to be faithful in the small things?
5. What unexpected keys might already be in your possession?
6. What has the process of waiting or searching revealed about your character?

Prayer to End the Chapter:

God, help me not to overlook what You've placed in front of me. Give me eyes to see the unexpected keys—the small assignments, the humble opportunities, the quiet moments of obedience. Teach me to trust that nothing is wasted and everything has purpose. Help me to steward what seems insignificant with excellence, knowing that it may be the very key to my next door. And when I find it, let me carry it with humility, knowing the greatest change often happens before the door even opens.

Amen.

Chapter 43: The Cost of the Open Door

Scripture:

"To whom much is given, much will be required." —Luke 12:48 **(NIV)**

Chapter Overview:

This chapter reminds readers that while we long for access and open doors, every door comes with responsibility. It explores the weight of walking through the very opportunities we prayed for and emphasizes the need for preparation, humility, and stewardship.

Chapter Content:

Everyone wants the door to open. We pray for it. Fast for it. Cry out for it. But rarely do we pause to consider what it will cost to walk through it.

Access is a blessing, but it's also a burden. An open door is not the finish line—it's the starting point of a new assignment, a new challenge, and a new level of responsibility.

When the door finally opens, you will be required to carry things you didn't carry in the hallway. You will be stretched in ways you weren't stretched in waiting. And you'll need to lean on God even more—not less—because elevation brings exposure.

That's why the preparation season is so important. It's not punishment. It's protection. It's the place where God builds the endurance, wisdom, and character you'll need once you walk through.

David didn't just walk into kingship; he was trained in the pasture. Joseph didn't step into the palace overnight; he was refined in prison. Esther didn't just become queen; she was prepared in obscurity. All of them had to carry the weight of an open door—and they could only do so because they were prepared in private.

You see, the door may open suddenly, but you must be steady.

With greater visibility comes greater responsibility. With greater favor comes greater accountability. And with every blessing comes a call to deeper obedience.

The open door will test your character. **Will you remain humble? Will you serve others or seek status? Will you still pray when everything is going well? Will you depend on God or grow comfortable in your success?**

That's the cost.

Sometimes the door opens and it looks glamorous from the outside, but what lies beyond it is a battlefield of balance—between purpose and pressure, between calling and compromise. The same hands you once lifted in surrender must now hold responsibility. The platform that once looked desirable becomes a place of discipline.

And this is why God doesn't just prepare you for access—He prepares you to ***carry*** what comes with it. He's not just shaping your gift—He's shaping your heart. Because it's your heart, not your hype, that sustains you behind the door.

If you neglect character in the hallway, you will collapse under the weight of the opportunity. But if you allow God to form you before He promotes you, you will not only rise—you will remain.

But it doesn't stop there.

The open door is not just for you. It's for everyone assigned to your obedience. It's for the people who will be encouraged by your journey, strengthened by your endurance, and equipped by your example.

You don't just walk through the door—you ***carry light*** through it. You bring hope, integrity, and leadership into spaces that were waiting for your voice, your heart, and your presence.

So as you wait, prepare. As you hope, grow. As you pray, trust. And when the door opens, step through with courage, remembering that it's not just about walking in—it's about walking well.

Key Points:

- Every open door comes with responsibility.
- Preparation in the hallway equips you for what's inside the room.
- Elevation will test what waiting has built in you.
- The blessing is not just about you—it's meant to serve others.
- Access should always be matched by stewardship.
- The open door is not just an opportunity—it's a responsibility to shine light and serve well.

Reflection Questions:

1. What are you doing right now to prepare for the open door you're praying for?
2. How has God used previous seasons to build your character?
3. Are there areas where you've desired elevation without preparation?
4. What does stewardship look like for the opportunity you're expecting?

5. How can you use future access to uplift others?
6. What internal disciplines must you develop now to sustain you after access is granted?

Prayer to End the Chapter:

Lord, thank You for the doors You've prepared for me. Help me to never take lightly the weight of walking through them. Grow my heart, my discipline, and my character so that I may carry access well. Keep me humble in elevation, faithful in responsibility, and anchored in Your presence no matter how high I rise. May every door I walk through bring glory to You and open the way for others to follow. Help me to be steady, not just successful. Surrendered, not just seen.

Amen.

Chapter 44: The Attack at the Threshold

Scripture:

"Put on the full armor of God, so that you can take your stand against the devil's schemes." —Ephesians 6:11 **(NIV)**

Chapter Overview:

This chapter explores the spiritual warfare that often intensifies right before breakthrough. It emphasizes the importance of recognizing and preparing for resistance that comes at the threshold of new access.

Chapter Content:

Right before the door opens, there's often a fight.

Have you ever noticed how intense things get just before something significant is about to happen? You were on the brink of a breakthrough—and suddenly, chaos hit your home. Discouragement overwhelmed your heart. Doubt crept into your mind. That's not coincidence—it's conflict.

The enemy doesn’t mind when you’re circling the hallway. But when you start aligning with God’s timing, walking in obedience, and preparing for purpose—that’s when he intensifies his attack. Because he knows what’s on the other side of your “yes.”

The threshold is sacred ground. It’s where faith is tested. It’s where fear tries to talk louder than purpose. It’s where resistance rises because promotion is near.

In the Bible, Nehemiah faced fierce opposition right as he was about to rebuild. Jesus faced temptation in the wilderness right before stepping into ministry. David encountered Goliath shortly before he was recognized as a warrior. These weren’t setbacks—they were threshold battles.

The attack at the threshold isn’t proof that you’re off course—it’s often confirmation that you’re on the verge of access.

The enemy doesn’t waste his energy where there is no potential. If you’re facing pressure, it’s because you’re approaching promise. If you're feeling surrounded, it may be because heaven is preparing to spotlight your next move.

But the key is this: don’t fight in your flesh. Fight in the Spirit. Put on the full armor of God. Speak truth when lies surround you. Stand firm when fear tries to shake you. Pray with power. Worship through the warfare. Refuse to retreat.

The closer you get to your breakthrough, the more strategic your resistance becomes. It's not just random. It's targeted. And it often comes in waves of discouragement, confusion, fatigue, or relational strain. The enemy will use familiar voices, unexpected delays, and personal vulnerabilities to try and derail your next step.

But God has already equipped you. The battle at the threshold is not just about access—it's about authority. It's about learning how to stand strong when the pressure increases and not shrink when destiny calls.

It's also about discernment. Not every closed door is a denial—and not every open door is divine. The attack at the threshold sharpens your discernment, increases your dependency on God, and anchors your heart in truth rather than emotion.

So don't be surprised when the heat turns up right before the release. The pressure is a sign. You're closer than you think.

The enemy may be roaring—but your faith can roar louder. Declare the promises of God. Guard your mind. Protect your peace. Keep your eyes on the door, and trust the One who holds the keys.

You've made it this far. Don't stop now. Your victory is on the other side of this test.

Key Points:

- Threshold battles often precede breakthrough.
- Resistance is often confirmation that access is near.
- Spiritual armor is essential at the door of opportunity.
- The enemy fights hardest when you're closest to destiny.
- Standing firm at the threshold is a declaration of spiritual maturity and readiness.
- Discernment is crucial at the threshold to recognize God's true doors.

Reflection Questions:

1. Have you experienced increased pressure right before a major breakthrough?
2. What tactics has the enemy used to distract or discourage you?
3. How can you intentionally **"armor up"** during moments of spiritual conflict?
4. What scriptures encourage you when you're under attack?
5. How can you stay focused on the door instead of the distractions around it?

6. What can you do today to strengthen your discernment and spiritual endurance?

Prayer to End the Chapter:

Lord, thank You for trusting me with access—even when it comes with opposition. Help me to stand strong at the threshold. Cover me in Your armor. Fill my heart with courage. Remind me that I am not fighting alone. I rebuke every distraction, every lie, every fear that tries to rise up. I declare that I am walking through this door by faith, with boldness and with spiritual authority. Strengthen my discernment. Anchor my heart. And give me grace to step forward even when resistance is great. Thank You for being my strength and my defender.

Amen.

Chapter 45: Walk Through Boldly

Scripture:

"The righteous are as bold as a lion." —Proverbs 28:1 **(NIV)**

Chapter Overview:

This chapter encourages readers to walk through open doors with holy confidence. After all the preparation, resistance, and refinement, there comes a moment where faith demands forward movement. This chapter is about courage, clarity, and obedience when the moment to step in finally arrives.

Chapter Content:

The door is open. You've waited. You've cried. You've grown. And now—it's time to walk through.

This is the moment you've prayed for, fasted for, and fought for. But stepping into the promise still takes courage. Sometimes, after all that anticipation, the step itself can feel intimidating.

But don't let fear delay you. Don't let doubt cause you to second-guess. God didn't bring you this far to abandon you at the entrance. You were built for this moment.

Boldness isn't the absence of fear—it's obedience in the face of it. It's saying yes when everything inside you whispers stay safe. It's trusting the One who opened the door more than the uncertainties on the other side.

Walking through boldly means letting go of the comfort zone. It means choosing calling over convenience. It's deciding that you won't shrink back or apologize for where God is taking you.

It means embracing your authority without arrogance and your calling without compromise. God doesn't give access so you can remain timid—He gives it so you can influence, build, and lead with conviction.

Boldness is not about noise—it's about knowing. Knowing that God has gone before you. Knowing that He walks beside you. Knowing that your identity is rooted in Him, not in your qualifications, performance, or public approval.

Sometimes walking through boldly means walking alone. Not everyone will understand the new space you're stepping into. Some people were only assigned to your hallway—not your destiny. That's okay. Don't hold back because others don't see what God showed you.

Boldness is a declaration of trust. It's stepping forward without having all the answers but knowing the One who holds them. It's refusing to delay destiny just because discomfort is knocking.

You've been stretched. You've been prepared. And now, boldness must become your default posture—not hesitation, not apology, but bold faith that walks with authority through the door God opened just for you.

So straighten your shoulders. Lift your head. And step in like you belong—because you do.

Key Points:

- Boldness is required to walk into answered prayers.
- Fear at the threshold is normal, but faith must lead.
- You don't need to feel ready to be ready.
- The door opened because God said so—not because you had it all together.
- Confidence comes from knowing who sent you, not what you see.
- Sometimes walking boldly means walking alone—and that's okay.

Reflection Questions:

1. What fears do you need to confront in order to walk through boldly?
2. What has God already proven to you about His faithfulness?
3. How can you walk in obedience even when you feel uncertain?
4. What does boldness look like for you in this season?
5. Who needs your example of courage to follow their own calling?
6. What mindsets or relationships might you need to release in order to step fully into this new season?

Prayer to End the Chapter:

God, I thank You for this open door. Help me to walk through with boldness, confidence, and faith. Silence every voice of fear and doubt. Let Your truth be louder than my hesitation. I trust that You've prepared me for this moment—and I won't let fear hold me back. I choose to move forward, knowing that You are with me, guiding me, and equipping me every step of the way. Give me grace for what's ahead, and boldness to walk like I belong in every room You've called me into.

Amen.

Chapter 16: When Access Feels Overwhelming

Scripture:

"My grace is sufficient for you, for my power is made perfect in weakness." —2 Corinthians 12:9 **(NIV)**

Chapter Overview:

This chapter speaks to the emotional and spiritual weight that can come after walking through the open door. It's the unexpected overwhelm of finally arriving—and realizing the pressure that comes with it. The message is clear: God's grace not only gets you through the door, but carries you once you're in.

Chapter Content:

You made it. The door opened. You walked through it. But now that you're on the other side, something unexpected is happening—you feel overwhelmed.

This is the part we don't often talk about. We celebrate the access. We honor the breakthrough. But we don't always prepare for the pressure that can follow.

The pressure to perform. The weight of responsibility. The fear of not being enough. The quiet voice whispering, ***"Can I really handle this?"***

Even after breakthrough, the enemy doesn't stop talking. If he can't keep you from access, he'll try to rob your peace once you've received it.

But here's the truth: grace didn't stop at the threshold. Grace walked in with you. God didn't bring you this far to let you fail under the weight of your calling. His strength is your foundation. His wisdom is your guide. His presence is your covering.

Overwhelm is a reminder to return—not to retreat, but to re-center. To lean into God again. To breathe deep and remember that you are not carrying this alone.

You weren't chosen because you were perfect—you were chosen because you were ***positioned***. God saw your faithfulness in the hallway. He honored your trust. And now He's walking with you through every challenge, every new responsibility, every stretching assignment.

Feeling overwhelmed doesn't mean you're out of place. It means you're growing. It means the environment is stretching you. And that's exactly what new territory is supposed to do.

Growth and discomfort go hand in hand. But grace meets you there.

Grace isn't just for the days when you're strong—it's especially for the days when you feel like you're not enough. It covers you when you doubt. It fills in the gaps when your strength runs low. It lifts you when your confidence is sinking under the weight of new responsibility.

Sometimes, access reveals areas of your life that still need healing. Sometimes it exposes insecurities you thought were behind you. But that's not to shame you—it's to shape you. God uses access not just to elevate you, but to mature you. And maturity often begins in the moments where you feel like you're sinking.

In those moments, don't isolate. Don't perform. Don't pretend. Invite God into the pressure. Invite Him into the overwhelm. He's not disappointed in your weakness—He's drawn to it. That's where His power shines the brightest.

So when the door opens and the weight settles in—don't run, and don't shrink. Acknowledge the pressure, but stand in His power. You are not alone in this new space. And what overwhelmed you at first will soon become the place where you thrive.

Because the same God who opened the door is the One who will keep you standing in the room.

Key Points:

- Access can come with unexpected pressure.
- Overwhelm is not failure—it's a signal to rely on God's grace.
- New doors stretch us, but they also grow us.
- You were chosen because you're positioned—not perfect.
- Grace will carry you through what obedience walked you into.
- God's power shows up strongest in places of weakness.

Reflection Questions:

1. Have you ever felt overwhelmed after a major breakthrough?
2. What expectations (from yourself or others) are you carrying right now?
3. How can you give yourself grace in this season of growth?
4. What practical steps help you return to God when you feel pressure rising?
5. What reminders or scriptures strengthen you when you feel weak?

6. What would it look like to truly trust God to carry what feels too heavy for you?

Prayer to End the Chapter:

Father, thank You for the doors You've opened. I admit that at times I feel overwhelmed by what's on the other side. Remind me that I'm not walking this alone. Help me to lean on Your grace, to rest in Your strength, and to release the pressure I put on myself. Teach me to grow without burning out, to lead without losing peace, and to serve from a place of being filled. Let Your presence steady me, and let Your power carry me. And when I feel like I'm not enough, remind me that Your grace always is.

Amen.

Chapter 47: New Room, New Rules

Scripture:

"See, I am doing a new thing! Now it springs up; do you not perceive it?" —Isaiah 43:19 **(NIV)**

Chapter Overview:

This chapter unpacks the importance of adapting to new environments and seasons. Access brings new expectations, new relationships, and new rhythms. What worked in the last season may not work here. This chapter helps readers embrace change and grow into the new level they've entered.

Chapter Content:

You're not in the hallway anymore. The door opened, and you've stepped into new space. But with every new room comes a new set of rules.

This can feel uncomfortable at first. You may find yourself trying to bring old habits, old mindsets, and old methods into a space that was never meant to operate under yesterday's patterns.

But here's the truth: new doors demand new discipline. What worked in the last season won't always sustain you in this one. God gave you access not so you could be comfortable—but so you could be transformed.

In this new room, there are different expectations. More visibility. Greater responsibility. And often, unfamiliar systems or relationships that require grace and wisdom to navigate.

This is where spiritual maturity steps in. Because now it's not just about getting in—it's about ***growing in***. Can you adjust your attitude when the environment requires more humility? Can you manage pressure without falling back into old coping mechanisms? Can you adapt without losing your authenticity?

It can be tempting to shrink back or default to what you know. But growth requires flexibility. Elevation demands adaptation.

Think of Joseph. The same wisdom that helped him interpret dreams in prison had to evolve when he managed Pharaoh's kingdom. His posture had to change. His language had to change. His leadership had to grow. He didn't lose who he was—but he had to grow into the version of himself that fit the new room.

You may have to adjust how you pray, how you manage your time, how you process feedback, how you lead, and how you rest. You may even need to create new boundaries to protect your peace and purpose.

And that's okay.

This is not regression—it's refinement.

Every new level God brings you to will stretch you to become more like Him. He's not just changing your scenery—He's shaping your spirit.

Don't fight the new rules. Learn them. Embrace them. Grow into them. Ask God to give you discernment, strategy, and humility as you navigate new expectations.

The truth is, staying in the room is just as much a miracle as getting in. Doors open through faith. But doors stay open through wisdom, obedience, and character.

You're not just walking through doors—you're learning how to stay in the room. And staying takes just as much grace as entering.

Key Points:

- Every new level requires a new level of discipline.
- Growth often means letting go of familiar methods.
- Elevation requires flexibility, humility, and discernment.

- New access brings new rhythms—and that's okay.
- Staying in the room requires transformation, not just talent.
- The grace that opened the door also empowers you to grow in it.

Reflection Questions:

1. What patterns or habits from your past season need to shift in this new space?
2. How have you resisted the "new rules" of your current environment?
3. What does spiritual maturity look like in this new room?
4. Are you willing to change your rhythm to grow into your next level?
5. What support or resources might help you navigate this transition wisely?
6. How is God using this new room to shape your character, not just your calling?

Prayer to End the Chapter:

Lord, thank You for the new space You've called me into. Help me not to cling to old patterns that no longer serve where You've placed me. Give me grace to grow, eyes to see what needs to change, and the humility to adjust. Let me not just enter this new room—but thrive in it. Shape my character, refine my habits, and deepen my wisdom. I trust that if You brought me here, You'll give me everything I need to stay, grow, and honor You in the process.

Amen.

Chapter 48: Closing One Door, Opening Another

Scripture:

"I have set before you an open door that no one can shut." — Revelation 3:8 **(NIV)**

Chapter Overview:

This chapter explores the sometimes painful reality of closing old doors as part of embracing the new. Letting go of familiar places, people, or roles can feel like loss, but it's often the gateway to new purpose. The chapter encourages readers to trust God's direction, even when transitions feel difficult.

Chapter Content:

Access isn't always just about stepping into something new—it's also about stepping ***away*** from something familiar.

Sometimes God opens a door by closing another. A job ends. A relationship shifts. A role you once thrived in no longer fits. And though you know deep down that something new is calling, part of you grieves what used to be.

That's normal. It's human to mourn what's ending, even when you're excited about what's next. But don't mistake closure for failure. Don't assume that walking away means giving up. Sometimes, it means growing up.

God doesn't close doors to hurt you—He closes them to make room. Room for the new rhythm, the new assignment, the next level of development and influence.

But the truth is, we often try to keep doors open that God is asking us to release. We stay out of comfort. We delay out of fear. We convince ourselves that what's familiar is better than what's ahead.

But access requires surrender.

You cannot enter the next room if you're clinging to the handle of the last one.

Letting go isn't always a loud, dramatic moment. Sometimes it's quiet. Sometimes it's a decision you make every day to stop returning to what no longer serves your growth.

That doesn't mean you forget where you came from. It means you bless it for what it taught you—and release it so you can walk forward freely.

Think of Abraham—called to leave everything familiar without even knowing where he was going. Or the disciples—asked to drop their nets, their jobs, their security to follow Jesus. The greatest journeys always begin with a step away.

This new door you're walking into may cost you some things—comfort, predictability, maybe even relationships—but what you gain will always outweigh what you leave behind.

God is not only the opener of doors—He's the sustainer of transitions. He holds you steady as you walk out of one chapter and into the next. And He promises that what's ahead is filled with purpose, peace, and provision.

Closure can feel like loss, but in God's hands, it becomes redirection.

So if you find yourself in a season of transition, where one door is closing and another is beginning to open, know this: you're not alone. And you're not off track. You are simply being led forward—guided by the hand of a God who writes endings with the same faithfulness He writes new beginnings.

Key Points:

- Access sometimes requires letting go of what's familiar.

- Closed doors are not failures—they're invitations to new growth.
- Transition can feel painful, but it's often the path to purpose.
- Holding on to the past can hinder your future.
- God's grace sustains you in every ending and every beginning.
- Surrender opens more doors than striving ever could.

Reflection Questions:

1. Is there a door in your life that God may be closing?
2. What fears are keeping you tied to what is no longer fruitful?
3. How can you honor your past without clinging to it?
4. What "next" is God trying to lead you into?
5. How can you welcome transition as a sacred part of your growth?
6. What might God be freeing you *for* by asking you to let go?

Prayer to End the Chapter:

God, help me to release what You've asked me to let go of. Give me peace when doors close and clarity for what lies ahead. Teach me to trust Your timing, Your wisdom, and Your love through every transition. Let me not fear what's next, but walk into it with hope, courage, and faith. Thank You for being with me in every ending—

and every beginning. Prepare my heart to say goodbye with gratitude and step forward with grace.

Amen.

Chapter 49: The Room Was Waiting for You

Scripture:

"For we are God's handiwork, created in Christ Jesus to do good works, which God prepared in advance for us to do." —Ephesians 2:10 **(NIV)**

Chapter Overview:

This chapter is a celebration of arrival—the moment when the reader fully realizes that the space they've stepped into was always prepared for them. It's an affirmation that they belong, they're equipped, and they're purposed for where they are. This chapter is about walking in full assurance and divine confidence.

Chapter Content:

You didn't stumble in by accident. You didn't break your way in. You were called, appointed, and assigned to this place. The room was waiting for you.

Every delay, every detour, every prayer in the hallway was preparing you for this moment. You belong here—not because of who you know, but because of Who called you. Not because you forced the door open, but because heaven authorized your access.

You might still feel nervous. That's okay. But don't let fear convince you that you're out of place. You are right where you're supposed to be.

God doesn't waste preparation. He doesn't extend invitations He doesn't mean. He's been shaping your capacity, maturing your character, and enlarging your vision for such a time as this.

The room you're in now might feel bigger than what you expected—but it's not bigger than your God. And He put you here on purpose, for purpose.

What's beautiful about divine placement is that it's not about comparison. You're not filling someone else's shoes. You're walking in the shoes that were made just for you.

There's room for your voice. Room for your gifts. Room for your leadership. And room for your growth. Don't shrink. Don't apologize. Show up fully—because the room was designed with you in mind.

And when you start to feel the weight of it all—remember, you're not carrying it alone. God's strength will meet you every day. His wisdom will guide your steps. His favor will open more doors as you walk faithfully in this one.

- You are not an imposter. You are anointed.
- You are not an outsider. You are ordained.
- You are not barely hanging on. You are deeply rooted in purpose.

The room was waiting for you. And now that you're here—bring your full self. Stand tall. Speak truth. Love well. Lead boldly.

Because your arrival isn't just about you—it's about the people who needed your presence, your influence, and your obedience.

And it's not just this room. There are more ahead. As you continue to walk in alignment with God's will, new doors will open, new rooms will be revealed, and new assignments will be given. But everything begins with the decision to stop doubting and start dwelling—in peace, in purpose, and in God's promises.

Celebrate this moment. Breathe it in. Thank God for it. Because what once felt out of reach is now your reality. And what once felt impossible is now part of your testimony.

So write in this space. Build in this space. Serve in this space. Don't just visit—***occupy***.

Because this room—this level, this season, this opportunity—wasn't a random occurrence. It was tailor-made. It has your name on it.

And now that you've arrived, the next chapter of impact begins.

Key Points:

- You didn't earn your way in—God prepared this place for you.
- Divine placement isn't accidental; it's intentional.
- You don't have to shrink in rooms that were built with you in mind.
- Confidence in your calling brings clarity to your purpose.
- Your presence in the room is a blessing to others, not just a reward for you.
- There are more rooms ahead, but this one requires your full presence and purpose.

Reflection Questions:

1. What have you overcome to get to this room?
2. How has God confirmed that you're right where you need to be?
3. What fears still try to make you feel unqualified?
4. How can you show up more fully in the space God has given you?

5. Who might be blessed by your obedience and presence in this room?
6. What legacy do you want to build in the room that was made for you?

Prayer to End the Chapter:

God, thank You for preparing this room for me. Thank You for every twist, turn, and waiting season that shaped me for where I am. Help me to walk with confidence, humility, and boldness. Silence every lie that says I don't belong. Remind me that this space was made for me—and I was made for it. Use me here. Stretch me here. Grow me here. Let this room become the place where Your glory is revealed through my obedience. And when the time comes to move to the next room, help me to go with peace, knowing You're already there too.

Amen.

Chapter 50: Access Granted

Scripture:

"Delight yourself in the Lord, and He will give you the desires of your heart." —Psalm 37:4 **(ESV)**

Chapter Overview:

This final chapter ties everything together. It affirms that access is not just about doors, but about identity. It's not just about the spaces you enter, but who you become in the process. ***"Access Granted"*** is not just a moment—it's a mindset. This chapter calls the reader to live boldly, purposefully, and confidently, knowing they are chosen, equipped, and sent.

Chapter Content:

You've prayed. You've waited. You've grown. You've walked through rejection, resistance, and refinement. And now, you've heard the words heaven has been whispering over you all along: ***Access Granted.***

Not just to a room. Not just to a role. But to a way of life rooted in faith, boldness, and divine authority.

Access is more than a reward. It's a responsibility. It's a call to live like you know who you are. It's walking in favor without arrogance. It's embracing elevation with humility. It's knowing that everything you've endured was not in vain—it was preparation for purpose.

- You didn't just survive. You were shaped.
- You didn't just endure. You emerged.
- You didn't just hope. You've been positioned.

Now it's time to walk like the door is already open. Because in Christ, it is.

Access Granted means you have the permission to be bold, the authority to lead, the assignment to serve, and the confidence to grow. It means you're no longer begging for validation—you're moving in revelation.

It means you stop disqualifying yourself based on your past and start declaring truth about your future.

Access Granted is about more than opportunity—it's about ownership. It's about stewarding what you've been given, building with what's in your hands, and believing that God will continue to make a way.

It's about understanding that you're not walking in someone else's blessing—you're walking in your own. What's for you is not a borrowed space. It's a place carved out by God for you to thrive, influence, and impact.

Access doesn't mean everything will be easy. It means you've been divinely endorsed to handle what's coming. You may still face resistance, but now you face it with authority. You may still encounter doubt, but now you walk in truth. You may still get tired, but now you move in grace.

You no longer have to ask, **"Am I worthy?"** You know that Jesus' sacrifice made you worthy. You no longer have to knock on doors hoping someone lets you in. Heaven already did.

So, build what you were born to build. Speak what you were called to speak. Live how you were created to live.

This isn't the end of the story. This is the beginning of a life that echoes the glory of the One who granted you access in the first place.

And here's the most powerful truth of all: your access is not just about ***you.*** It's about the legacy you're creating. The people you'll lift. The doors you'll open for others. The trail you're blazing so someone else can follow.

So keep moving forward. Keep trusting. Keep building. Because what's ahead is still unfolding—and God's not finished with you yet.

Access has been granted. Now walk in it.

Key Points:

- Access is not just about rooms—it's about identity and purpose.
- God grants access to those He's prepared and positioned.
- Walking in access requires confidence, humility, and stewardship.
- You are not waiting for permission—you've already been approved.
- Your life is a reflection of the One who granted you access.
- The access you've received will bless others for generations to come.

Reflection Questions:

1. What does ***"Access Granted"*** now mean to you personally?
2. How have you been changed by the journey of walking through doors?
3. In what ways will you begin to walk in new boldness starting today?

4. What will you build or create with the access you've been given?
5. How will you help open doors for others as you continue to grow?
6. What legacy of access are you preparing to pass on?

Prayer to End the Chapter:

Lord, thank You for granting me access. Thank You for every lesson, every delay, every breakthrough that led me to this moment. I choose to walk in confidence, not fear. I choose to live from identity, not insecurity. Help me to steward this access well—to love, to lead, to serve, and to build for Your glory. I declare that I am chosen, equipped, and ready. Access has been granted, and I will never live the same. Use my life to open doors for others, and let Your light shine through everything I do.

Amen.

7-Day Devotional: Living the Access Granted Life

Day 1: Positioned on Purpose

Scripture: Jeremiah 1:5

Reflection: You are not an accident. Every part of your journey—every high and low—has been preparing you for where you are. God doesn't waste seasons.

Prayer: Lord, help me embrace the truth that I was created with intention.Let me trust Your timing and plan.

Prompt: Write one way God has used your past to position you for the present.

Day 2: Walk Through Boldly

Scripture: Joshua 1:9

Reflection: Courage isn't the absence of fear; it's choosing faith anyway. You've been equipped to move forward.

Prayer: God, give me the boldness to step into what You've called me to, even when I feel afraid.

Prompt: Where is God calling you to move boldly today?

Day 3: Leaving the Old Behind

Scripture: Isaiah 43:18–19

Reflection: Growth requires release. What was good for a past season may no longer serve this one.

Prayer: Father, give me the strength to let go of what You've asked me to release.

Prompt: What is something you're holding onto that God is asking you to surrender?

Day 4: Steward What's in Your Hands

Scripture: Luke 16:10

Reflection: Big blessings start with faithful stewardship of small things.

Prayer: Lord, help me to honor the opportunities You've already given me.

Prompt: What's in your hand right now that you can maximize?

Day 5: Grace to Remain

Scripture: 2 Corinthians 12:9

Reflection: The same grace that brought you through the door will sustain you in the room.

Prayer: God, strengthen me in the places where I feel weak. Let Your grace carry me.

Prompt: Where do you need God's strength the most in this season?

Day 6: Prepare the Way for Others

Scripture: Proverbs 11:25

Reflection: Your access is never just for you—it's also for those who will come behind you.

Prayer: Lord, help me use my influence to uplift and empower others.

Prompt: Who is one person you can encourage or mentor today?

Day 7: Access Granted, Purpose Activated

Scripture: Romans 8:28

Reflection: God is weaving every detail together for your good and His glory. It's time to activate your purpose.

Prayer: Father, thank You for trusting me with this life. Help me to live it fully, boldly, and for You.

Prompt: What is your next step toward living your "Access Granted" purpose?

A Letter to the Reader

Dear Reader,

If you've made it to this point, thank you. Thank you for turning each page, for reflecting on each chapter, and for allowing your heart to remain open to God's voice along the journey. This book wasn't just written—it was lived, prayed over, and birthed through seasons of waiting, breakthrough, and deep trust.

"Access Granted" isn't just a title. It's a testimony. And now it belongs to you too.

My prayer is that something within these chapters stirred a holy confidence inside of you. That you now see your life through the lens of purpose. That you no longer wait passively at closed doors but walk boldly through the ones God opens, knowing that you are called, prepared, and more than enough in Him.

You have access—not because of perfection, but because of grace. You are qualified—not by resume, but by His Spirit. And you are ready—not because you have all the answers, but because God walks with you step by step.

Whatever season you're in—whether you're still in the hallway or you've just stepped into the room—I want to remind you: You are seen. You are loved. You are needed. And the world is better because of your **"yes."**

Let this book be more than a moment. Let it be a movement in your heart. Let it remind you of who you are and whose you are.

Access has been granted. Now go and live like it.

With gratitude and expectation, **[Author's Name]**

Notes

(For your thoughts, prayers, and personal reflections as you walk out your "Access Granted" journey.)

www.ingramcontent.com/pod-product-compliance
Lightning Source LLC
LaVergne TN
LVHW012048160826
845678LV00014B/2745

9798999994257